Insight Study Guide

Grace Moore

A Christmas Carol

Charles Dickens

insight

insight

Charles Dickens' A Christmas Carol by Grace Moore
Insight Study Guide series

Copyright © 2011 Insight Publications Pty Ltd

First published in 2011 by
Insight Publications Pty Ltd
ABN 57 005 102 983
89 Wellington Street
St Kilda VIC 3182
Australia
Tel: +61 3 9523 0044
Fax: +61 3 9523 2044
Email: books@insightpublications.com
Website: www.insightpublications.com

This edition published 2011 in the United States of America by
Insight Publications Pty Ltd, Australia.

ISBN-13: 978-1-921411-91-5

Library of Congress Control Number: 2011931334

Cover Design by The Modern Art Production Group
Cover Illustrations by The Modern Art Production Group,
istockphoto® and House Industries
Internal Design by Sarn Potter

Printed in the United States of America by Lightning Source
10 9 8 7 6 5 4 3 2 1

contents

CHARACTER MAP

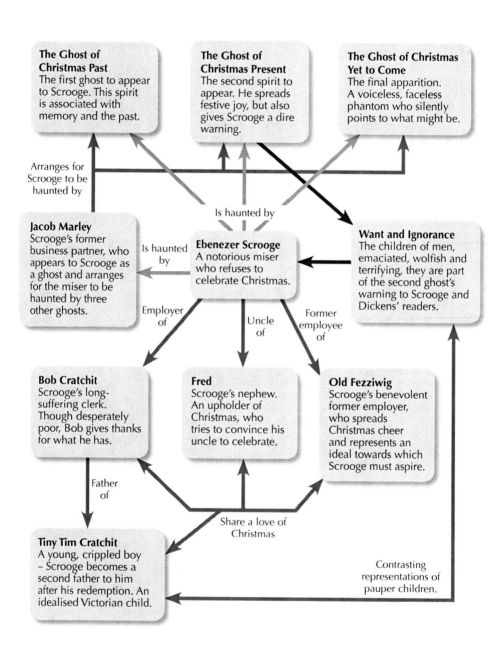

The Ghost of Christmas Past
The first ghost to appear to Scrooge. This spirit is associated with memory and the past.

The Ghost of Christmas Present
The second spirit to appear. He spreads festive joy, but also gives Scrooge a dire warning.

The Ghost of Christmas Yet to Come
The final apparition. A voiceless, faceless phantom who silently points to what might be.

Arranges for Scrooge to be haunted by

Is haunted by

Jacob Marley
Scrooge's former business partner, who appears to Scrooge as a ghost and arranges for the miser to be haunted by three other ghosts.

Is haunted by

Ebenezer Scrooge
A notorious miser who refuses to celebrate Christmas.

Want and Ignorance
The children of men, emaciated, wolfish and terrifying, they are part of the second ghost's warning to Scrooge and Dickens' readers.

Employer of

Uncle of

Former employee of

Bob Cratchit
Scrooge's long-suffering clerk. Though desperately poor, Bob gives thanks for what he has.

Fred
Scrooge's nephew. An upholder of Christmas, who tries to convince his uncle to celebrate.

Old Fezziwig
Scrooge's benevolent former employer, who spreads Christmas cheer and represents an ideal towards which Scrooge must aspire.

Father of

Share a love of Christmas

Tiny Tim Cratchit
A young, crippled boy – Scrooge becomes a second father to him after his redemption. An idealised Victorian child.

Contrasting representations of pauper children.

OVERVIEW

About the author

Charles John Huffam Dickens was born in Portsmouth, England in 1812. His father, John Dickens, worked as a pay clerk for the royal navy, although his personal finances were rather fraught. John Dickens was known as a generous, convivial man, but he struggled with debt for much of his adult life and in 1824 he was imprisoned in the Marshalsea Debtors' Prison.

Charles Dickens was only twelve years old at the time of his father's arrest and was sent to work at Warren's Blacking Factory, where he was employed to fix labels onto bottles of boot blacking. A deeply sensitive young man, Dickens found the experience to be both threatening and degrading, and he seems never to have truly recovered. John Dickens secured his release from the Marshalsea Prison in May 1824, but his son continued to work at the blacking factory until the father argued with the owner, several weeks later. The trauma of this sudden descent from a middle-class childhood to the world of work never left Dickens, although in his lifetime he confided only in his friend, John Forster, who eventually became his biographer. Dickens never forgave his mother for her eagerness to patch up the quarrel with the factory owners and send her son back to work.

This brief taste of poverty undoubtedly shaped the rest of Dickens' life. It provided him with a remarkable drive to succeed, but it also gave him insight into the miseries of the urban underclass and particularly the sufferings of poor children. Dickens returned to school for a brief spell, but was then apprenticed as a clerk to a firm of solicitors. Not finding the legal profession to be stimulating, he went on to work as a parliamentary reporter, regularly writing up accounts of debates (including those surrounding child labour) for newspapers.

Bubbling over with ambition and energy, Dickens also began to write short fictional sketches and submitted one of these to the *Monthly Magazine* in 1832. The piece was not only accepted, its author was commissioned to produce more and these short works were eventually collected as *Sketches by Boz*. In 1836, Dickens was approached by the publishers Chapman and Hall to provide the text for a set of sporting illustrations by the artist Robert Seymour. As Dickens gained more creative control of the project, the characters developed and gradually *The Pickwick Papers* was born. Early sales were disappointing and Seymour, who had been battling depression for some time, committed suicide in April 1836. Dickens, however, seized the opportunity to reshape the work. *The Pickwick Papers* became an immense success and from this point onwards Dickens was regarded as an up-and-coming novelist of great talent.

Synopsis

A Christmas Carol is a difficult novella to classify, and according to Juliet John it has become a 'cultural myth' providing 'a parable for the modern, commercial age' (John, p.270). Certainly, the story continues to resonate almost two centuries after its first appearance, and this is partly because it remains desperately relevant in a socially and economically divided world. For some readers it is a ghost story, for others a time-travel narrative and for others still, it is an exposé of social inequality in 1840s Britain. The story revolves around the miser Ebenezer Scrooge, a ruthless businessman who cares for nobody and who exploits his impoverished clerk, Bob Cratchit. Known only for his penny pinching, Scrooge is visited by the ghost of his late business partner, Jacob Marley, who walks the earth as a spirit forced to carry a chain representing the sins of his life. Marley warns Scrooge that he will share this fate unless he mends his ways and tells him that he will be visited by three ghosts.

The first ghost to appear is the Ghost of Christmas Past, who shows Scrooge scenes from his boyhood. The ghost plays on Scrooge's nostalgia, but also shows readers that Scrooge was neglected by his father and often forced to remain at school while his fellow students returned home for the holidays. The ghostly visions gradually become more serious, as Dickens shows Scrooge becoming increasingly obsessed with material wealth at the expense of human relations. The next ghost is the Ghost of Christmas Present, who begins by showing Scrooge cheerful festive scenes, including an impoverished but merry Christmas in the Cratchit household. As with the first spirit, though, the yuletide celebrations gradually give way to darker visions, and Scrooge learns that his clerk's small, crippled son Tiny Tim will die unless someone aids the Cratchit family. After a harrowing scene in which Scrooge is confronted with the children of men, Want and Ignorance, the ghost vanishes and Scrooge finds himself in the presence of the Ghost of Christmas Yet to Come.

Unlike the other two spirits, the third ghost is silent, leaving Scrooge to supply the narrative and draw his own conclusions. The ghost shows Scrooge the most chilling of all of the visions. Scrooge hears a range of discussions regarding a recently dead man about whom nobody has a kind word to say. Gradually, he realises that he is seeing a vision of his own future and that *he* is the unpleasant miser whose death is being celebrated by his creditors and employees. Juxtaposed with the revelry surrounding Scrooge's death is the deep sorrow of the Cratchit family, whom we see mourning the loss of Tiny Tim. The ghost then takes Scrooge to his own graveside where, in terror, he pledges, 'I will not be the man I must have been but for this intercourse' (p.108). As he pleads with the spirit for another chance, the ghost gradually transforms into Scrooge's bedpost and the miser finds himself in his own home.

Resolved to keep his promise, Scrooge responds with great emotion and energy to the opportunity he has been given to change his life. He arranges for a prize turkey to be sent to the Cratchits (as John Sutherland points out, in contrast to the meagre goose with which they celebrate in the Ghost of Christmas Present's vision of their Christmas meal). He then goes to his nephew's house and, after years of declining his invitations, joins him and his family for Christmas dinner. The story ends with Scrooge informing Bob Cratchit that he will raise his salary and assist his family, while the narrator informs us that Tiny Tim did not die and that Scrooge became an exemplary man who was never again visited by spirits.

Character summaries

Characters are listed here in order of appearance.

Ebenezer Scrooge: a notorious miser and misanthropic moneylender, who refuses to recognise or celebrate Christmas.

Jacob Marley: Scrooge's former business partner. Like Scrooge, a miser who appears as a ghost to warn his former partner that he must mend his ways.

Fred: Scrooge's cheerful, generous nephew, the son of Scrooge's sister *Fan*. Fred has for many years attempted to persuade his uncle to celebrate Christmas with him.

Bob Cratchit: Scrooge's long-suffering clerk. Scrooge pays Bob a pittance and forces him to work in a freezing office. In spite of his exploitative work conditions, Bob remains a cheerful and loving husband and father, who is grateful for small mercies.

The Two Gentlemen: collecting money for charity, these men are appalled by Scrooge's callous attitude to poverty and his refusal to assist those in need. One of the two gentlemen returns as 'the portly gentleman' in the closing pages.

The Ghost of Christmas Past: the first of three spirits to visit Scrooge. The Ghost of Christmas Past takes the miser back to his childhood and scenes from his life as a young man to remind him of a time when he cared for people rather than money.

Fan: Scrooge's younger sister. Appears in Scrooge's recollection of his boyhood to bring Ebenezer home from school, having persuaded their father to allow the boy to come home for the holidays. The Ghost of Christmas Past tells us that Fan dies a young woman and is the mother of one son, Scrooge's nephew, *Fred*.

Old Fezziwig: Scrooge's employer when he is a young apprentice. A kind, generous man, Fezziwig provides memorable Christmas festivities for his family and those in his employment.

Belle: Scrooge's former fiancée, who releases him from a long engagement because of his growing avarice and worldly ambition.

The Ghost of Christmas Present: A 'jolly Giant' (p.72) who spreads good cheer at Christmas, particularly to those in need. He reveals a number of Christmas celebrations to Scrooge, including those of his nephew and the Cratchit family. He also introduces the miser to Want and Ignorance.

Mrs Cratchit: The loyal wife of Bob, Mrs. Cratchit is a loving parent who manages her meagre household budget as well as she can. She refutes Bob's affection for Ebenezer Scrooge, initially refusing to engage in a Christmas toast to the miser.

Tim Cratchit (Tiny Tim): Bob's weak youngest son, Tim is doomed to die unless his family's living conditions improve. Like Bob, Tim is cheery and thankful. He is most memorable for his joyful enjoinder, 'God bless Us, Every One!'

Want and Ignorance: Presented to Scrooge as the children of man, these two terrifying figures represent humanity's future if people fail to respond to the plight of the poor. Almost wild in demeanour, the children have been neglected to the point that they have become feral.

The Ghost of Christmas Yet to Come: The most sinister of all the spirits. We never see this ghost's face, nor do we hear him speak. His terrifying visions are of what the future will be if Scrooge refuses to reform.

Old Joe: A dealer in used goods who buys Ebenezer Scrooge's belongings from his employees in the Ghost of Christmas Yet to Come's vision. He lives in a particularly unpleasant area of the city.

Charwoman; Mrs Dilber; the undertaker's man: Three characters who steal and sell Scrooge's possessions to *Old Joe*.

BACKGROUND & CONTEXT

Historical setting

Writing at a time when the balance of political power in Britain had shifted from the landed gentry to the manufacturing middle classes, Dickens wanted to rally the public into action. The Great Reform Bill of 1832 had given many male middle-class property owners the right to vote for the first time. While the aristocracy had long believed in the idea that with noble birth came responsibility (*noblesse oblige*), those who had risen to social dominance through their own hard work as factory owners or captains of industry generally did not share this belief, subscribing instead to the idea that with enough effort anyone could succeed. Like his great friend and mentor, the writer and philosopher Thomas Carlyle, Dickens was deeply agitated by what he perceived as the inertia of the wealthy middle classes. Dickens' opinion was that those with riches and influence had a duty to take care of those who were less fortunate than themselves, particularly since their wealth was often founded on the labours of a poorly paid workforce. Dickens was to be a lifelong critic of this negligence, condemning it most witheringly in *Little Dorrit* (1855–1857).

In *A Christmas Carol*, Dickens continued the deep commitment to social reform he had begun in novels like *Oliver Twist* (1837–1839) and *Nicholas Nickleby* (1838–1839), both of which sought to expose poverty and privation. In *Nicholas Nickleby*, Dickens exposed the notorious Yorkshire Schools and their scandalous treatment of the children who were abandoned to them. Unwanted or illegitimate children were sent away to these schools by people who never wanted to see them again. Many of the children died, while those who survived were kept in sub-human conditions. In *Oliver Twist*, Dickens hit out at the *Poor Law Amendment Act*, which had done away with the system of parish relief, whereby paupers were given aid so that they could remain in their own homes. In the past, those who had fallen on hard times were encouraged to live among their neighbours and to get themselves back on their feet with the support of the community. This relatively humane system was replaced by the workhouses.

Purported to be charitable institutions, workhouses centralised the distribution of aid and provided those in need with a roof over their heads and a (paltry) food allowance. They were perceived by many members of the governing classes as a deterrent to idleness, but they rapidly became a source of terror to the poor, who regarded them as akin to prisons. Working people lived in fear of having to resort to 'the house'. Conditions within the workhouses were horrific – starvation and abuse were rife, and those with authority frequently sought to punish inmates for their misfortune. Dickens uses the relationship between the miser and his clerk to draw attention to the enormous gap between the living conditions of masters and their workers, carefully emphasising the human element of the story by allowing the reader to enter into Bob's happy home and to see his family's daily struggles to make ends meet.

Author's historical context

Dickens seems to have enjoyed the writing of *A Christmas Carol* immensely. On 2 January 1844, he wrote to a friend:

> Charles Dickens wept, and laughed, and wept again, and excited himself in a most extraordinary manner, in the composition; and thinking whereof, he walked about the black streets of London, fifteen and twenty miles, many a night when all the sober folks had gone to bed (*Letters*: 4, 2).

It was unusual for Dickens to express this much pleasure in the creative process. All too frequently in his career, he was writing in installments and up against a deadline, but his commentary here suggests that the shorter format of the novella – a work longer than a short story, but shorter than a novel – suited him.

While he may be exaggerating about the distances he walked, Dickens frequently took to the streets when he was working on a project and unable to sleep, and he often gained inspiration by wandering through the slum areas and observing them. Certainly, there are graphic scenes towards the novella's close that demonstrate Dickens' first-hand experience of the capital city's seedier side, and it is likely that his forays into the most neglected areas of London strengthened his resolve that the work would deal a blow for reform like a 'Sledge hammer' (*Letters*: 3, 459), as he promised a fellow social reformer, Dr Thomas Southwood Smith.

A Christmas Carol appeared at the beginning of the decade that came to be known as the 'Hungry Forties', a period that encompassed the catastrophic Irish potato famine, as well as intense suffering for the English working classes. Part of Dickens' aim as a novelist strongly committed to social reform was to make his comfortable middle-class readers aware of the poverty and degradation around them. Social conditions in Britain in the 1840s were so markedly divided that the novelist and politician Benjamin Disraeli notoriously referred to his country as made up of 'two nations, the rich and the poor' in his novel *Sybil* (1845).

A number of different social concerns occupied Dickens' attention as he began to conceive of the novella. His friend John Forster believed that a visit to the industrial manufacturing city of Manchester in October 1843 provided the impetus for Dickens to write *A Christmas Carol*. Among his many commitments in the city, Dickens spoke at a fundraising event for the Manchester Athenaeum, an institution offering educational opportunities to working men. In his speech, Dickens addressed the need to provide education for the poor, suggesting that the right to learn was comparable with the need to eat, asserting at one point, 'Though he should find it hard for a season even to keep the wolf of hunger from his door let him but once have chased the dragon of ignorance from his hearth' (in Fielding, p.48).

The connection between education and poverty was certainly a prominent concern for Dickens as he worked on his little Christmas book. There were other issues troubling the author, however. In September, for instance, Dickens had visited a 'ragged school' (an institution offering evening classes and religious instruction for those living in extreme poverty) at Field Lane in Holborn. Dickens undertook the visit as a representative of his friend, Angela Burdett Coutts, an extremely wealthy philanthropist who often called on the novelist to advise her at this time.

He wrote to Miss Coutts on 16 September in terms that evoke the language and imagery he would soon use so effectively in *A Christmas Carol*:

> On Thursday night, I went to the Ragged School; and an awful sight it is ... I have very seldom seen, in all the strange and dreadful things I have seen in London and elsewhere, anything so shocking as the dire neglect of soul and body exhibited in these children. And although I know; and am as sure as it is possible for one to be of anything which has not happened; that in the prodigious misery and ignorance of the swarming masses of mankind in England, the seeds of its certain ruin are sown, I never saw that Truth so staring out in hopeless characters, as it does from the walls of this place. The children in the Jails are almost as common sights to me as my own; but these are worse, for they have not arrived there yet, but are as plainly and certainly travelling there, as they are to their Graves (*Letters*: 3, 562).

Dickens was obviously horrified by the atrocious conditions in which these children were somehow expected to learn and he saw clearly that no child could be expected to develop into a responsible adult with this kind of start in life. Dickens was equally shocked by two early versions of the parliamentary reports of the Children's Employment Commission, which he had received in December 1840 and February 1843 respectively. While he had initially pledged to write an article or pamphlet 'on behalf of the poor man's child', promising several times to produce an article for the *Edinburgh Review,* he later determined to channel his efforts into fiction, rather than a factual account, and *A Christmas Carol* was born.

Publishing context

A Christmas Carol was something of an experiment for Dickens and he had high hopes for its commercial success. It was the first of his popular Christmas books and it remains, without doubt, Dickens' best-loved festive tale. Dickens originally produced the story as a rapid way of clearing a debt with his publishers Chapman and Hall. Visually, the novella was stunning and obviously designed to be a Christmas gift. The book was beautifully bound and incorporated colour plates and woodcuts by the artist John Leech. Aesthetically pleasing though the book was, production costs ate into Dickens' profits. The initial print run of six thousand copies sold out within a matter of days, yet Dickens made only two hundred and thirty pounds from the venture (Schlicke, p.98).

GENRE, STRUCTURE & LANGUAGE

Genre

The work's title should alert us to Dickens' own sense of how it should be perceived. It is, somewhat paradoxically, a 'Carol in Prose', suggesting a light, musical theme, but it is also, according to its subtitle, 'A Ghost Story of Christmas'. In some respects, Dickens was engaged in creating his own genre in writing *A Christmas Carol*. The novella was the first of a sequence of 'Christmas Books' Dickens produced in the 1840s. Ruth Glancy has argued that these small volumes (*The Chimes*, 1844; *The Cricket on the Hearth*, 1845; *The Battle of Life*, 1846 and *The Haunted Man*, 1847) 'changed the course of English publishing' (in Schlicke, p.97). Dickens later wrote of what he called his '*Carol* philosophy' (*Letters*: 4, 328), thus demonstrating his comprehension of his work's remarkable impact upon his culture and its understanding of Christmas.

A Christmas Carol is partly a Christmas morality tale, in which evil is exposed, virtuous characters (like the Cratchits) are rewarded, and everyone celebrates at the conclusion. There are, of course, issues raised by the novella that remain unresolved. The sinister children of men, Want and Ignorance, do not go away just because Scrooge has been reformed, but the narrator tells us nothing of their future and the work's wider social critique quietly fades away.

Dickens' decision to politicise his first Christmas book was fraught with risk, and it is a testament to his skill in balancing the cheerful with the bleak that the work was so well received by his readers. It is therefore hardly surprising that he limits the work's true terror, by refusing to dwell on society's enormous social divisions. While Christmas is traditionally regarded as a time to think of those who are not so fortunate, it is also a time when readers wish to escape from their day-to-day responsibilities. Dickens therefore had to measure his novella's narrative tone very carefully, taking care not to articulate his broad political arguments too forcefully.

The Gothic

Its important social commentary aside, *A Christmas Carol* is also a thrilling ghost story that is, at times, chilling and terrifying and at others side-splittingly funny. Dickens carefully blends realism and the supernatural to create a world in which the Gothic and the mundane sit side by side. Much of Dickens' early writing drew upon Gothic conventions, and although he was primarily a realist writer, he interwove Gothic tales into novels including *The Pickwick Papers* and *Nicholas Nickleby*. Following the publication of Horace Walpole's *The Castle of Otranto* in 1764, the Gothic genre became a highly popular form; Dickens was certainly familiar with the work of Gothic novelists including Ann Radcliffe and Matthew Lewis. Eighteenth-century Gothic writing was highly formulaic and often remarkably melodramatic. The action usually took place in a labyrinthine castle or house and often involved a virtuous and vulnerable heroine fleeing a number of apparently supernatural horrors. Jane Austen ruthlessly parodied the absurdity of Gothic conventions in *Northanger Abbey* (1818), and although Gothic novels themselves fell out of fashion until a revival of interest towards the end of the nineteenth century, novelists including Dickens often drew upon Gothic conventions in order to sensationalise their writing.

With its dark, chilly setting and its supernatural visitors, *A Christmas Carol* certainly draws on elements of the Gothic novel. Thus, Scrooge's door-knocker can turn into Jacob Marley's face, and the reader will accept this as a reality within the limits of the story. The narrator provides a number of descriptions in which Gothic elements are interwoven with freezing, icy imagery to emphasise the atmosphere of mystery and to remind us of the protagonist's icy heart:

> The ancient tower of a church, whose gruff old bell was always peeping slily down at Scrooge out of a Gothic window in the wall, became invisible, and struck the hours and quarters in the clouds, with tremulous vibrations afterwards, as if its teeth were chattering in its frozen head up there. (p.39)

The tower and the bell, imported directly from the eighteenth-century Gothic novel, instantly convey the darkness and fear to follow. They also provide a superb contrast with the Christmas morning scenes, which are notable for their crisp brightness. Dickens adapts the Gothic, using it intermittently in his descriptions, and juxtaposing it with the real.

Structure

The structure of A Christmas Carol is very different from any of Dickens' other works prior to the 1840s, and his decision to write a novella reflects an understanding of the need for a piece of short, light reading during the festive season.

In terms of its internal structure, the story is particularly concerned with time, to the extent that it can be considered a time-travel narrative. Dickens is somewhat cavalier with the constraints of the clock, as the ghosts somehow truncate their visitations into a single night, while moving backwards and forwards in time. Scrooge goes to bed at two o'clock, yet as he waits for the first ghost, he hears the clock strike midnight (p.53). Scrooge awakens to see the second ghost at one (p.71), which is at the same time as the first spirit finally appears, but then the clock strikes twelve again (p.94) when the last spirit materialises. Scrooge then awakes to realise that somehow the ghosts have compressed their visions into a single night (p.112). Dickens' playful attitude towards time blurs the boundaries between the real and the imaginary, while at the same time highlighting the mysterious otherworldliness of Scrooge's encounter.

Aside from the ghostly visitors, the work is skilfully organised so that Dickens' readers move between its important socio-political message and the festive hilarity in which some of its more lovable characters engage. It is divided into five 'staves' – like a song – suggesting a lightness that is belied by some of its content. While the three main visitations take place in the middle of the story, scenes from Scrooge's current life, before and after his conversion, frame his supernatural adventures with the ghosts, who embody different aspects of Christmas.

It is significant that the Ghost of Christmas Present sits at the very centre of the novella. Part of Dickens' message is a call for people to live in the present and to take care of those around them, rather than hoarding up wealth for an indefinite future. Postponing this most vocally critical of the spirits to the middle stave also allows Dickens to begin with a festive tone, before giving way to forceful social indictment. Then, through the device of the silent ghost, he leaves his readers to offload their guilt, responsibility and anxieties onto the narrative gap left by the spirit's uncanny voicelessness. Lest the reader is overwhelmed by the graphic depiction of the 'surplus population' and their foetid living conditions, Dickens then shifts back to celebratory mode in the novel's final stave, restoring the festive atmosphere, while emphasising that even a man as removed from society as Scrooge can be redeemed.

Language

According to Michael Slater, the tone of A Christmas Carol is that of a 'jolly, kind-hearted bachelor uncle, seated across the hearth from his hearers on some festive occasion' (Slater, 1969, p.20). The story's opening and closing passages certainly suggest a convivial narrator who is telling the tale to a group of close friends. Thus, the voice speaks of 'our ancestors' (p.33, author's italics), digresses to talk about coffin nails and brings the story to a close with a pun on the word 'spirit', when he speaks of the 'Total Abstinence Principle' (p.118). This approach sets the tone for a Christmas ghost story, but does not prepare the reader for some of the terror to follow, or for the novella's stern moral message.

Notwithstanding the almost jocular tone that surrounds the three chapters in which Scrooge is haunted, Slater's comments downplay the force of some of the more sinister characters and the language they invoke. The first ghost is gentle and, aside from introducing his various visions, he has very little to say. The Ghost of Christmas Present, however, is a much more imposing figure. While he begins in a beneficent, jovial manner, as his time on earth grows shorter, his words become increasingly urgent and condemnatory. He foreshadows a future in which the neglected underclass will rise up to seize the basic comforts it has been denied. His vocabulary is appropriately bleak as he predicts the 'Doom' ahead (p.94). So powerful are this spirit's words, that in the next stave, the faceless Ghost of Christmas Yet to Come is denied language altogether, depending only on eerie gestures and the reader's imagination to generate his meanings, in a creative masterstroke through which Dickens forces readers to project their own terror onto the phantom.

Scrooge's own language undergoes a remarkable transformation between the beginning and the end of the story. When we first encounter him, Scrooge's favourite expression is the dismissive 'Bah! ... Humbug!' (p.35), with which he rejects any talk of charity or Christmas cheer. His speech is limited to necessary communications and when he is away from his office, eating dinner in a tavern, he is completely silent. The force of Scrooge's words is emphasised through the growls and snarls with which he delivers them (p.37). However, once he has been redeemed by the spirits' ghostly visions, his language changes as rapidly as his personality. His speech becomes effusive, punctuated by laughter and expressions of joy. He also incorporates simile and metaphor into his exclamations, comparing himself to an angel, a feather and a schoolboy all in one breath (p.111) and talking endlessly of his happiness about the second chance he has been offered.

CHAPTER-BY-CHAPTER ANALYSIS

Preface (p.28)

Although it is extremely brief, Dickens uses the preface to set up a contrast between the work's seasonal humour and levity and the 'Ghost of an Idea', which is its broader message about a shared humanity and responsibility. Dickens' assertion, 'May it haunt their house pleasantly, and no one wish to lay it', suggests that he expects the story to have an afterlife and that its spirit will linger in the home, perhaps providing a lesson to readers. Dickens' hope that the idea will not put his readers out of humour 'with themselves, with each other, with the season, or with me' demonstrates his careful attempt to balance entertainment and didacticism so that his readers will learn from the story without feeling that Dickens has introduced misery into the festive season.

Stave One (pp.33–52)

Summary: *The reader is introduced to Ebenezer Scrooge, a notorious miser and misanthrope, who refuses to celebrate Christmas and who treats everyone around him with excessive meanness. Scrooge is visited by the ghost of his former business partner, Jacob Marley, who tells him that he must mend his ways. Marley warns Scrooge that he will be visited by three ghosts on three separate nights.*

Dickens sets the scene with the chilling opening words, 'Marley was dead' (p.33), establishing the authority of his omniscient narrator and introducing Scrooge's misanthropy by showing his indifference to his partner Jacob Marley's death. The narrator's tone is amiable and familiar – almost chatty – and Dickens presents the voice as akin to that of a storyteller, digressing to talk about Hamlet's father and using strategies including repetition to create the impression that we are listening to the spoken word, rather than reading words on a page. For the Victorians, reading aloud was much more of a communal activity than it is today and the novella's length meant that it could easily be read aloud in one sitting.

Having made readers aware of Scrooge's callous nature, Dickens emphasises his cold-heartedness by showing how his physical features have warped along with his character:

> Hard and sharp as flint, from which no steel had ever struck out generous fire; secret, and self-contained, and solitary as an oyster. The cold within him froze his old features, nipped his pointed nose, shrivelled his cheek, stiffened his gait; made his eyes red, his thin lips blue; and spoke out shrewdly in his grating voice. A frosty rime was on his head, and on his eyebrows, and his wiry chin (p.34).

Here, Dickens alerts us to the convergence between physical appearance and character which plays an important part in the story. Scrooge's physique reflects his lack of personal warmth and while we learn that the weather outside is snowy and delightfully festive, Scrooge's coldness penetrates to much greater depths. His personal iciness is contrasted with the efforts of the people who are outside and trying to keep warm, while the gloom of his office is set against the bright candles burning in the windows of other establishments.

Once he has established the self-imposed solitude of Scrooge's distrustful life, Dickens then begins to introduce the other characters, beginning with Bob Cratchit, Scrooge's clerk, whose working conditions are so appalling that we see him attempting to warm himself with a candle. The arrival of Scrooge's nephew Fred provides a clear contrast between the miserly businessman and his good-humoured relative, as Fred attempts to spread Christmas cheer. When Scrooge ridicules Fred's improvident marriage, he shows his rejection of the Victorian ideal of the family, which has been displaced for him by the accumulation of riches.

It is on Fred's departure, however, that one of the work's most significant concerns is brought to light. Bob Cratchit admits the two gentlemen who are collecting to provide some Christmas cheer for the destitute. When Scrooge demands, 'Are there no prisons?' (p.38) he aligns himself with the practice of Utilitarianism, the philosophy that upholds the doctrine of 'the greatest happiness of the greatest number' (see THEMES, IDEAS & VALUES).

Key point

A long-time critic of Jeremy Bentham (the founder of Utilitarianism) and the application of his ideas to social policy, Dickens uses Scrooge as a mouthpiece to expose the brutality of interning paupers in a workhouse, rather than providing for them in a compassionate manner. Scrooge's outright refusal of aid is an extreme reaction, designed to shock readers out of their inertia, which is as dangerous as Scrooge's hostility.

Up to this point, the tone of the narrative has been realistic, but when Scrooge leaves his office, Dickens gradually shifts genres, moving from realism to a supernatural tale. The narrator draws attention to Scrooge's solitary life by showing him dining alone, taking his 'melancholy dinner' in his 'usual melancholy tavern' (p.41). When Scrooge goes home, Dickens prepares the reader for the ghostly scenes to follow by accumulating dark and Gothic imagery. Scrooge's rooms (inherited from Marley) are 'gloomy' and tucked away and, on this night, covered in frost and fog; descriptions that reinforce their occupant's misery. We learn that Scrooge is the only person to make his home in the building and that he rents the other rooms out to businesses. The fact that Scrooge has converted his building into a commercial property points to a contempt for the sanctity of home and a refusal to build a private life away from the world of work. He is at odds with his society's emphasis on the importance of the family and its separation of the world into two spheres: the public world of work and the private realm of the home, the latter usually presided over by a supportive, 'angelic' wife.

The scene's growing gloom gradually prepares the reader for Scrooge's surprise and uncertainty as his door-knocker and then his fireplace metamorphose into Marley's face. As Marley appears, Dickens conveys Scrooge's horror, but also shows that the miser's incredulity has given way to belief in the ghost and the warning he brings. When Scrooge looks out of the window to see a host of chain-wearing phantoms, many of whom were known to him in life, he points to one of the central warnings at the heart of A Christmas Carol. The ghosts he sees are all disempowered, doomed to watch suffering for eternity, but unable to intervene or offer help. While up to this point in the narrative readers are appalled by Scrooge, when he stands at the window Dickens invites us to share his perspective and to identify with his terror and curiosity. Like Scrooge, we should be afraid of becoming powerless spectators; we should move from merely reading to taking action before it is too late.

Q How does Dickens set up a contrast between Scrooge and his clerk, Bob Cratchit?

Q Examine some of the descriptions of the people on the streets (e.g. on pp.39–40) and consider how Dickens represents working people and their Christmas celebrations.

Q Why does Scrooge want to compress the ghosts' visits into one night, rather than spreading them across three?

Stave Two (pp. 53–70)

Summary: Having resolved that his experience with Marley was just a dream, Scrooge awakens to the chimes of midnight and is visited by the first spirit, the Ghost of Christmas Past. The ghost takes Scrooge back to his childhood, where the miser reveals both pity and nostalgia for himself as a boy. The scene changes to a Christmas party, thrown by Scrooge's former employer, Old Fezziwig, before transforming again to an encounter between Scrooge and his fiancée, Belle, who breaks off their engagement because Ebenezer has become too obsessed with wealth. We then see Belle later in life, happy with a husband and children, and learn that Jacob Marley is on the brink of death. Scrooge then extinguishes the spirit's light and falls asleep.

Scrooge awakes, wondering whether he has slept through an entire day. He feels puzzled by his experiences and wonders whether he has been dreaming – a question that is never fully resolved at the end of the story. When the Ghost of Christmas Past arrives, Scrooge is struck by the strangeness of his appearance, with aspects of him moving into and out of focus, and a bright jet of light protruding from his head, at times visible and at others dull. The spirit's movement between haziness and distinctness aligns him with the memories he represents, some of which are more vivid than others.

Scrooge is clearly threatened by the ghost and the memories he evokes, which might explain why he begs the spirit to cover his light. The pair then walk through a wall and find themselves in a scene from Scrooge's boyhood. Scrooge responds emotionally to the place and is particularly struck by its smells; 'He was conscious of a thousand odours floating in the air, each one connected with a thousand thoughts, and hopes, and joys, and cares long, long, forgotten!' (p.57). The aromas evoke Scrooge's long suppressed memories and, although he denies it, he is moved to tears. As he sees people wishing one another a Merry Christmas, Scrooge is strangely moved by the experience and, although he doesn't consciously register it, he recaptures some of his boyhood glee and excitement for the festive season.

When the ghost tells Scrooge that a single lonely child remains at the nearby school, the miser responds with great emotion and weeps for his abandoned younger self. On seeing a vision of Ali Baba (p.58) through a window, Scrooge recounts a boyhood Christmas visitation from a number of well-known literary figures. Harry Stone has commented that the visual experience of not just recalling, but actually seeing his boyhood fantasies enables the miser to remember his childhood (Stone, p.16). Indeed, the scene where the adult Scrooge watches his younger self retreating into an imaginary world is one of the most pathos-laden incidents in the entire novella.

Key Point

Scrooge weeps with pleasure and sorrow at the memories of his childhood loneliness, and of the imaginative attempts he made to flee his solitude. This scene also marks the beginning of Scrooge's rehabilitation, his first movement towards restoring his lost compassion and empathy, as he connects his memory of himself to a more recent incident in which he rudely dismissed a young carol singer from his door (p.40).

In returning to this early period of loneliness, we are invited to see Scrooge's potential for reform, but also the reasons for his decline into a life of miserable isolation. Dickens shows us Scrooge's neglected childhood in order to help us understand the forces that have shaped him, but also to help us as readers to make the link between the miser and the many abandoned children on the streets of Victorian Britain. Dickens' broader, more subtle point here is that neglect can only result in misery and upheaval, not just for those who are in need of aid, but also those who turn a blind eye to the troubles of their fellow human beings.

The scene then shifts to a different Christmas; Scrooge is still at school, but he is older and no longer reading. His young sister, Fan, comes to collect him, telling him that their stern father is much kinder than before and that Scrooge will join his family for a merry Christmas. Dickens sets up a contrast between little Fan's light giddiness and the terrible austerity of Scrooge's school, which is as cold and unwelcoming as Scrooge's adult home. When the ghost reflects on Fan's kindness and reminds Scrooge of her son, his nephew Fred, Scrooge becomes quiet and ponderous. However, before he has a chance to reflect on the many invitations from Fred that he has spurned, the ghost transports Scrooge to another Christmas scene.

Scrooge now observes his first experiences in the world of work, revisiting the scene of his apprenticeship and one of the extravagant Christmas parties thrown by his employer, old Mr Fezziwig. Like the Ghost of Christmas Present, whom we meet in the next stave, Fezziwig is a larger-than-life figure, too big for his high desk and calling out in a 'comfortable, oily, rich, fat, jovial voice' (p.61). The sight of Fezziwig transports Scrooge into the emotional state he occupied as a young man, and he responds to the vision of his former employer with uncharacteristic pleasure. The scene is a convivial one, with joyful dancing, drinking and eating and Old Mr Fezziwig is unstoppable in his merry-making. The ghost then mimics the contemptuous voice of the older Scrooge, downplaying the significance of Fezziwig's revelry because it has only cost a small sum of money. Scrooge responds indignantly, revealing the power of an employer to shape his workers' lives. He declares:

> He has the power to render us happy or unhappy; to make our service light or burdensome; a pleasure or a toil. Say that his power lies in words and looks; in things so slight and insignificant that it is impossible to add and count 'em up: what then? The happiness he gives, is quite as great as if it cost a fortune (p.64).

Key Point

Voicing his support for the joy Old Fezziwig spreads, Scrooge begins to realise that he has some responsibility for Bob Cratchit's happiness.

The scene then changes again, with the ghost warning Scrooge that they must hurry, as his time on earth grows short. Scrooge sees himself this time as a slightly older man, and his countenance has taken on the appearance of greed. We see a heart-rending exchange between Scrooge and his fiancée, Belle, in which she releases him from their long-standing engagement, because she knows that he has changed. Valuing money more than love, Scrooge has deferred their marriage until more prosperous times, but gradually his pursuit of wealth has become all-consuming. Belle tells him how greatly he has changed, and Scrooge responds defensively, arguing that he has never sought release from their engagement and making his terror of poverty evident.

Key Point

Dickens adds complexity to Scrooge's character by showing readers that his miserliness has grown from a fear of poverty.

The ghost responds violently to Scrooge's exhortation not to see any further shadows, forcing him to observe the next scene, which is of an older Belle, with her happy, boisterous family. The love between Belle and her husband is obvious, as is the affection shared by the family. Belle's husband then mentions that he has seen Scrooge, whose partner Marley is dying, leaving Scrooge alone in the world. Overwhelmed by these scenes, the miser struggles with the spirit, desperately trying to shut out his light, before finding himself in bed and falling into a deep sleep.

Q Why might Dickens set up a contrast between the warm and the cold, the light and the darkness?

Q How does Dickens use windows and what Scrooge sees through them to frame the narrative?

Q Why does the Ghost of Christmas Past fluctuate in his appearance and distinctness?

Q Why is it important for Scrooge to feel pity for his younger self?

Q Why does Scrooge want to extinguish the ghost's light?

Q How is nostalgia for the past connected with Scrooge's later reform?

Stave Three (pp.71–94)

Summary: *Scrooge awakes at the stroke of one to find that his room has been transformed into the scene of a feast by the Ghost of Christmas Present. The ghost takes Scrooge to see a number of festive gatherings, including that of the Cratchit family, where Scrooge is moved to pity by the sight of Bob's crippled son, Tiny Tim. Having shown him what he is missing, the ghost then introduces Scrooge to Want and Ignorance, the children of man. The ghost quotes some of Scrooge's draconian pronouncements back to him, before disappearing. As the clock strikes twelve, the final spirit appears.*

Scrooge awakens, poised for another ghostly encounter and, paradoxically, when no ghost appears, he begins to tremble. He sees a supernatural light in the next room, however, and eventually decides to follow it. A voice urges him to enter, and finds the room laden with food and festooned with decorations. Scrooge meets the 'jolly Giant' (p.72), the Ghost of Christmas Present, a figure who is remarkably unfamiliar to him. The miser, though, admits that he has learned from his interactions with the Ghost of Christmas Past and that he will endeavour to learn from this new encounter. Scrooge touches the ghost's robe and is transported to the city streets on Christmas morning, where he sees joyful revelry. This stave is notable for its many depictions of food and feasting (for instance p.72 and pp.75–77), showing the distinctions between Christmas meals prepared for the wealthy and those made by the poor, as well as the shared jubilation that transcends class boundaries. Dickens contrasts the cold of the snow with the warmth of the hearth and presents Christmas as a type of antidote to the chilling winter weather. The narrator tells us, 'There was nothing very cheerful in the climate or the town, and yet there was an air of cheerfulness abroad that the clearest summer air and brightest summer sun might have endeavoured to diffuse in vain' (p.75).

The spirit shows himself to be particularly concerned with the welfare of the poor, sprinkling incense on their dinners as they scurry to the bakers' shops and restoring good cheer between those who have quarrelled. When Scrooge asks the ghost what he is sprinkling, the spirit explains that he is adding his own 'flavour' to the proceedings. Even though this is obviously a dose of good humour, Scrooge proceeds to berate the spirit for depriving the people of 'opportunities of innocent enjoyment' as well as 'their means of dining every seventh day' (p.77). The ghost is initially astonished by Scrooge's allegations that he is a Sabbatarian (someone who believes that the Sabbath should be a day of complete rest, a problematic ideal in a world where working people received few holidays and lacked the facilities to cook food in their own homes). He explains to Scrooge that those who claim to act in his name do not always represent Christian values and that the truly good should not be held responsible for the actions of selfish impostors.

Scrooge and the ghost move through the town, spreading happiness and sympathy for the poor. They eventually arrive at Bob Cratchit's home, where Dickens contrasts the family's jollity with the extreme poverty in which they live, identifying them clearly as members of the thrifty poor – hard-working, law-abiding people who often lived in wretched conditions, but who made the best of what they had. Scrooge sees the Cratchits enjoying a pitifully meagre Christmas lunch and he witnesses Bob's tender treatment of his small, crippled son, Tiny Tim. Once again, the narrator offers lavish descriptions of the feast (pp.80–81), but in this instance they are laden with pathos because there is scarcely enough food to go around.

Moved by Tim's condition, Scrooge asks the spirit whether he will survive to adulthood and, quoting his own Malthusian words back to him (see THEMES, IDEAS & VALUES), the ghost explains that the boy will die unless the future is changed.

Key Point

Scrooge is filled with guilt when he hears his callous words applied to Tim's condition and hangs his head with shame, demonstrating that he is continuing to learn from the ghosts.

Dickens accentuates his point here by moving directly to an exchange between the Cratchits in which Mrs Cratchit initially refuses to drink Scrooge's health, but gives way for her husband's sake and because it is

Christmas. Scrooge observes the Cratchits for some time further, before he is transported to a number of other Christmas scenes, both within cities and in remote areas, including a lighthouse. Regardless of their geographical isolation, everyone he sees is celebrating in some way and this provides an unspoken lesson to Scrooge, who has always spurned the festive season. Importantly, many of the revellers also draw on happy memories of Christmases of old, pointing to the way in which Scrooge has separated himself from his past until he is forced to confront it by his ghostly visitors.

When Scrooge suddenly finds himself at his nephew's house, he is struck by the good humour of Fred, his wife and their guests, but he is also dismayed to find that he is a topic of conversation. While Fred expresses bemused sympathy with his uncle, his wife is indignant at Scrooge's unwillingness to participate in any type of seasonal revelry. Fred declares that he will continue to invite Scrooge for Christmas dinner, in the hope that one day it will make an impression upon him. The conversation then gives way to music, and Scrooge is deeply affected by the sound of his niece playing the harp (p.89). His memories are stirred and the sound of a familiar song takes him back to his school days, evoking a more recent memory of the Ghost of Christmas Past. Scrooge watches the games and merriment for a while longer, enjoying the vision, before the spirit takes him to view sick-beds, poverty, people overseas and those in prison, all celebrating.

Key Scene

Just as Scrooge is speaking with the spirit about the shortness of his life, he sees what he thinks is a claw emerging from his skirts. The spirit produces two emaciated children, who are clearly starving, degraded and envious. The children are in direct contrast to the piety of Tiny Tim and the other Cratchits and are shockingly distinct from the compliant infants who usually feature in realist novels. The children have been reduced to the status of animals and, following so rapidly from the jovial scenes of celebration, they shock the reader and terrify Scrooge. The genial spirit's voice undergoes a sudden shift in tone, as he uses the starkest possible language to explain mankind's culpability for the children, Want and Ignorance. Using phrases like 'Slander those who tell it ye!' (p.94), the ghost's language sounds increasingly prophetic, becoming almost biblical as he attacks the petty factions within established religions that prevent action to help those who need it most. When Scrooge asks what can be done to assist, the ghost turns on him and, once again, repeats the miser's unfeeling question from the first stave, 'Are there no prisons? ... Are there no workhouses' (p.94). Each time this question is repeated, it sounds increasingly cold and sinister. Dickens skilfully condemns Scrooge via Scrooge's own words, without needing to provide an extensive moral commentary that would sit awkwardly in a story written for Christmas time.

> **Q** Why are there so many depictions of food and eating in this stave? Take a look at some of the descriptions and examine the language Dickens uses when he writes about food.
>
> **Q** Do you respond emotionally to the sentimental language surrounding Tiny Tim? Why or why not?
>
> **Q** Why is Scrooge moved by music?
>
> **Q** Why does the ghost show Want and Ignorance to Scrooge? Do you find it incongruous that the most convivial of all the spirits makes this introduction?

Stave Four (pp.95–110)

Summary: Scrooge expresses terror in the presence of the Ghost of Christmas Past, whose face is hidden. The ghost takes Scrooge to a scene in which a charwoman, a laundress and an undertaker's man visit a dealer in second-hand goods in order to sell items they have plundered from a recently dead man. Scrooge asks to see some joy connected with death and is transported to a scene where an impoverished husband and wife express happiness that their ruthless creditor has just died and cannot foreclose on their debt. Asking to see some tenderness connected with death, Scrooge is shown the Cratchit family mourning the recently dead Tiny Tim. Scrooge goes on to ask about the dead man whose belongings were being sold. The ghost takes Scrooge to the graveyard and silently points to a grave. When Scrooge looks down, he sees his own name and begs for mercy, catching the spirit's hand, which transforms into a bedpost.*

Scrooge is approached by a totally silent and faceless phantom, whose lack of features compels the reader to draw upon her or his worst nightmares to fill in the gaps. The miser experiences a 'vague uncertain horror' (p.95) when he is with the ghost. Nevertheless, he tells him to lead on. The ghost takes him to the 'Change' [the stock exchange, where Scrooge does business] where he hears that an unnamed man has died and that nobody will attend the funeral.

Key Point

Having been able to connect his experiences with the two previous Ghosts directly back to his own life, Scrooge is mystified by this vision. He searches for himself (pp.97–98), believing that if he is able to see himself in the future, he will receive the moral lesson that will help him to improve.

The ghost leads Scrooge to an unfamiliar area of the city, where the poverty and squalor is overwhelming:

> The ways were foul and narrow; the shops and houses wretched; the people half-naked, drunken, slipshod, ugly. Alleys and archways, like so many cesspools, disgorged their offences of smell, and dirt, and life, upon the straggling streets; and the whole quarter reeked with crime, with filth, and misery (p.98).

This description is in direct contrast to the neat shabbiness of Bob Cratchit's poor home and points to an even more wretched form of poverty stemming from neglect and decay. Although the narrator does not make the connection explicit, areas of this type are what the Victorian popular novelist Watts Philips described as the 'nurseries of crime' that give rise to wolfish, self-interested children like Want and Ignorance if they are not taken in hand.

Scrooge finds himself in a second-hand goods shop, observing a charwoman, a laundress and an undertaker's man, all attempting to sell items they have stolen from a recently dead man. Scrooge is horrified by the group's callous behaviour as he watches the man and two women produce everything from blankets, to a pilfered burial shirt, while the narrator reinforces the atrocity of the scene by describing them as akin to, 'obscene demons, marketing the corpse itself' (p.102). Scrooge believes the vision to be a warning, but still recoils when the ghost urges him to look at the man's corpse, alone beneath a ragged sheet. The miser asks if there is anyone in London who feels emotion connected to the man's death, and the ghost takes him to a room where he sees a man and a woman rejoicing because their creditor is dead. While the couple will not be relieved of their debt, they believe that no other creditor will treat them as harshly as the unnamed dead man.

Despairing of seeing any positive responses to this man's death, Scrooge asks the ghost to show him some tenderness connected with mortality. The spirit takes him once more to the Cratchit household, but this time it is eerily silent and the previously boisterous family are sombrely seated around the fire. The Cratchits are in mourning for Tiny Tim and waiting for Bob, who has been visiting his little son's grave. Although the house is decorated for Christmas, the upstairs room is filled with reminders of Tim and Bob takes solace in them. When he returns downstairs, Bob mentions that Scrooge's nephew, Fred, has offered to help the family and they all speculate as to whether the eldest son, Peter, might be offered a better position. The fact that they anticipate Fred's assistance will take the form of a new post points to the industriousness of the Cratchits – they are not looking for any unearned assistance, rather for ways in which they may help themselves.

The ghost and Scrooge then hurry away to the churchyard. The ghost refuses to answer any of Scrooge's questions about whether the future is absolutely determined, or whether it can be changed, instead eerily pointing to a gravestone, which bears Scrooge's name. On learning that he is the man for whom nobody can mourn, Scrooge begs to know whether he still has a chance to change. The spirit's hand trembles slightly, possibly indicating that Scrooge still has a chance to reform, yet when Scrooge grabs it, the hand attempts to free itself. Scrooge pledges to honour Christmas and to assimilate what he has learned from each Christmas into his life. As he begins another impassioned plea, the ghost is suddenly transformed into a bedpost, which diminishes the terror of this haunting chapter and allows Dickens to shift genres back from a ghost story to a Christmas tale.

Key Point

Scrooge promises to 'live in the Past, the Present and the Future' (p.111) and to embody the spirit of each of the three Ghosts.

Q The first two Ghosts have been vocal. What effect does Dickens achieve by rendering the Ghost of Christmas Yet to Come silent?

Q Do you think that the Ghost's sudden metamorphosis into a bedpost is an effective conclusion to the stave? Draw upon the text to explain why or why not.

Stave Five (pp.111–118)

Summary: *Scrooge awakes, still holding the bedpost and expressing delight that he is not dead. He throws open his window and ascertains that it is Christmas Day. Scrooge sends a boy to a butchers' shop to buy the prize turkey and take it to the Cratchits' home. Scrooge then wanders about the streets, encountering one of the two gentlemen whose charitable efforts he rebuffed earlier, and offering him a sizeable donation. To everyone's surprise, he also attends Fred's Christmas dinner. The next morning he greets Bob who is late, in his usual curmudgeonly manner, but swiftly changes his demeanour and offers to increase his salary.*

The concluding stave allows Dickens to provide his readers with the type of 'happy ending' they would expect and demand from a festive story. Scrooge may awaken holding onto his own bedpost, suggesting that the whole experience may be a dream, but his subsequent conduct demonstrates that he is committed to reforming his character and takes the hauntings seriously.

Scrooge's behaviour in these concluding pages is boyish and a little absurd, as he whoops and laughs and continually exclaims 'Oh, glorious. Glorious!' (p.112). This rapid transformation from abrupt miser to effusive benefactor stretches the reader's credulity, reminding us that we are reading a Christmas fantasy, rather than the type of realist writing for which Dickens was becoming famous. Scrooge's generosity towards the Cratchits in sending them the prize turkey is in sharp contrast to his miserly conduct in the past and some readers may find this rapid change difficult to accept.

Q Are you willing to believe that Scrooge is a changed man? Draw upon the text to explain why or why not.

CHARACTERS & RELATIONSHIPS

In approaching Dickens' characters, it is worth taking the time to examine the illustrations by John Leech that accompany the text. Dickens was heavily involved in the illustrative process, offering advice and feedback, and often making exacting demands for revisions. The illustrations therefore reflect the characters as he envisaged them, and there is an unusually strong connection between the written and the visual in Dickens' work as a whole.

Ebenezer Scrooge

Key quotes

Merry Christmas! Out upon merry Christmas! What's Christmas time to you but a time for paying bills without money; a time for finding yourself a year older, and not an hour richer; a time for balancing your books and having every item in 'em through a round dozen of months presented dead against you? If I could work my will … every idiot who goes about with "Merry Christmas," on his lips, should be boiled with his own pudding and buried with a stake of holly through his heart (p.36).

'Are there no prisons? (p.38)

'I will live in the Past, the Present, and the Future!' (p.111)

Scrooge represents the worst characteristics of his society. Fixated with material goods at the expense of all human connection, particularly with his beleaguered clerk, Bob Cratchit, Scrooge is an allegorical embodiment of the forces of capitalism underpinning Britain's economy in the 1840s. For Dickens, he represented everything that was wrong with society in an increasingly industrialised world where human relations took second place to profits. Scrooge is completely alienated from his society when the novella opens. By positioning the miser on the margins of society, observing the festivities from which he has cut himself off, Dickens cleverly contrasts the life of the selfish, lonely man with the childlike delight of characters like Bob Cratchit and Old Fezziwig.

While Scrooge's reform tests the reader's credulity, the insights Dickens provides into his early life help us to understand that he is not an intrinsically bad character; rather he is fearful and damaged. Dickens himself had experienced a brush with poverty and even during his most prosperous and successful years he still worried about money and how to provide for his large family. It is perhaps for this reason that Dickens offers us insights into the miser's past, showing that as a young man Scrooge was afraid of how the world would respond if he were to fall into poverty. His comment to Belle on the inconsistency of his society's attitude to wealth is revealing: 'There is nothing on which [the world] is so hard as poverty; and there is nothing it professes to condemn with such severity as the pursuit of wealth' (p.65). As we observe Scrooge responding to events from his younger days, we gradually see that he is far from an evil character. His quest for wealth has been the result of a childhood of neglect and abandonment and a terror of being left to the mercy of an indifferent society.

Jacob Marley

Key quotes

'I wear the chain I forged in life … I made it link by link, and yard by yard; I girded it on of my own free will, and of my own free will I wore it.' (pp.47–48)

'You will be haunted … by Three Spirits.' (p.50)

Marley's primary role in the text is to show to Scrooge what he may become. Although he does not appear in any of the scenes showing Scrooge's past, he has obviously been an influence on Scrooge, who declares 'You were always a good man of business' (p.49) and 'You were always a good friend to me, Jacob' (p.50). Marley's appearance as a spirit is a source of great terror to Scrooge, who is terrified both by the chain Marley has forged and by his pitiful expressions of remorse and helplessness. Marley seems to feel an ongoing connection with his former partner: he tells Scrooge that he has sat by him 'many and many a day' (p.49) and he has engineered Scrooge's chance for redemption.

Bob Cratchit

Key quotes

> The office was closed in a twinkling, and the clerk, with the long ends of his white comforter dangling below his waist (for he boasted no great-coat), went down a slide on Cornhill, at the end of a lane of boys, twenty times, in honour of its being Christmas-eve, and then ran home to Candem Town as hard as he could pelt, to play at blindman's-buff (p.41).
>
> 'I'll give you Mr. Scrooge, the Founder of the Feast!' (p.83)

Bob Cratchit represents the virtuous, deserving poor and sits at the story's moral centre. He works hard, he is inexplicably loyal to Scrooge and he is a kind, loving husband and father. He bears some resemblance to Old Fezziwig, in that he is wholehearted in his celebration of Christmas, but he is nowhere near as prosperous as Scrooge's former employer. Curiously, even though Bob has little money of his own, the narrative voice directly compares him to coinage when it asks us to 'Think of that! Bob had but fifteen "Bob" a-week himself; he pocketed on Saturdays but fifteen copies of his Christian name; and yet the Ghost of Christmas Present blessed his four-roomed house!' (p.78). This pun on Bob's name emphasises his extreme poverty and also echoes Scrooge's earlier inadvertent admission of the inadequacy of his employee's salary when he exclaimed, 'my clerk, with fifteen shillings-a week, and a wife and family, talking about a merry Christmas. I'll retire to Bedlam.' (pp.37–8). Uninterested in worldly goods, Bob is the embodiment of the perfect Victorian worker, content in his family and happy with his lot.

In spite of his poverty, Bob is able to evoke the spirit of Christmas without depending on material trappings. We know from his behaviour and from the narrator's observations that Bob is a noble man who works hard for a ruthless master who threatens to dismiss him when he applauds Fred's defence of Christmas (p.37). At no point in the narrative does he threaten to leave his post, or display envy towards his mean yet wealthy master. Interestingly, while for today's readers Scrooge is regarded as the story's central character, as Catherine Waters notes, this was not always the case. Rather than Scrooge, Dickens' first readers saw 'the Cratchit family as the heart of the book, and dramatic adaptations during the

Victorian period often assigned the lead role to Bob Cratchit rather than Ebenezer Scrooge' (Waters, p.76).

The centrality of Bob and his family to this story and to Scrooge's reform reflects the emphasis the Victorians placed on the home and reinforces Scrooge's terrible isolation.

Fred

Key quotes

'I am sorry for him; I couldn't be angry with him if I tried. Who suffers by his ill whims! Himself, always.' (p.87)

'He may rail at Christmas till he dies, but he can't help thinking better of it – I defy him – if he finds me going there, in good temper, year after year, and saying Uncle Scrooge, how are you?' (p.88)

Fred is a character best aligned with Bob Cratchit and Old Fezziwig for his ability to celebrate Christmas. Generous and fun-loving, he is also a man of great persistence, as is evidenced by his annual invitation to his Uncle Scrooge for Christmas dinner. Fred cares for those less fortunate than himself, hoping that Scrooge may eventually leave Bob something in his will and, in the vision of Christmas Yet to Come, offering to help the Cratchits in any way he can. Fred is a reminder to Scrooge of the past from which he has alienated himself, as he is the only son of the miser's sister, Fan. It is only when Scrooge can reconcile himself to his history, allowing his memories back into his life, that he is able to connect with Fred and to attend his Christmas festivities.

The Ghost of Christmas Past

Key quotes

'"Spirit!" said Scrooge, "show me no more! Conduct me home. Why do you delight to torture me?"' (p.66)

The first of the spirits is associated with memory; his showing Scrooge a sequence of scenes from his boyhood and his years as a young man serves a dual purpose. On the one hand, he reveals that Scrooge has not always been the man he is now, but that neglect and fear have gradually transformed him. On the other, he helps Scrooge to remember times of both loneliness and joy, emotions from which he has retreated out of a misplaced sense of self-preservation. This Ghost is the least judgmental of the three and by comparison has very little to say as he takes the miser from vision to vision. Scrooge is both attracted to and troubled by him and, in particular, he is eager to extinguish to spirit's flame, eventually struggling with him and pressing his extinguisher down on his head. The spirit's light seems to symbolise memory, and the scene demonstrates the inescapability of our past recollections. Try as he might, Scrooge is unable to shut out the Ghost's light, which streams out from beneath the cap and illuminates the miser to the point of exhaustion.

Old Fezziwig

Key quotes

> He has the power to render us happy or unhappy; to make our service light or burdensome; a pleasure or a toil. Say that his power lies in words and looks; in things so slight and insignificant that it is impossible to add and count 'em up: what then? The happiness he gives, is quite as great as if it cost a fortune (p.64).

Old Fezziwig is one of the novella's most genial characters, embodying the spirit of Christmas. Unlike the older Scrooge, Fezziwig knows how to celebrate and is not challenged or confronted by involving his employees in the festivities. The vision of his ball is a pivotal moment for Scrooge, prompting him to remember how to enjoy himself, as well as recognise that his treatment of Bob has been unacceptable. If Bob Cratchit is a model employee, then Fezziwig is an ideal employer.

Belle

Key quotes

> 'Another idol has displaced me; and if it can cheer and comfort you in time to come, as I would have tried to do, I have no just cause to grieve.' (p.65)

> 'Our contract is an old one ... You *are* changed. When it was made, you were another man.' (pp.65–6)

The scene between Scrooge and Belle is one of the most moving in the novella. Although she only appears in two visions, Belle is presented as a beautiful, compassionate young woman, as she breaks off her engagement to Ebenezer. This encounter shows how Scrooge has begun to change, but it also reveals that his need to hoard money may have stemmed from fear. Importantly, while Scrooge responds to the broken engagement by becoming more obsessed with wealth, we see Belle in the second vision as a happy older woman, showing no trace of bitterness and taking pleasure in her family.

The Ghost of Christmas Present

Key quotes

'Come in! and know me better, man!' (p.72)

'If these shadows remain unaltered by the Future, the child will die.' (p.82)

Will you decide what men shall live, what men shall die? It may be that in the sight of Heaven, you are more worthless and less fit to live than millions like this poor man's child. Oh God! To hear the Insect on the leaf pronouncing on the too much life among his hungry brothers in the dust! (p.82)

A curiously changing spirit, the Ghost of Christmas Present begins as the least confronting of all the phantoms, but his character gradually changes during the course of the visitation. When Scrooge first encounters him, the ghost is clearly identified with the Christmas cheer he helps to spread. He is connected to food and abundance, and he shows particular compassion for the poor, helping to infuse their paltry Christmas meals with joy. The visit to the Cratchit household, however, marks a turning point at which the ghost's tone changes and becomes much more accusatory. The spirit begins to echo Scrooge's words back to him, showing the miser how inhumane the abstract principles behind Malthusianism and Utilitarianism are when they are applied to real people (see THEMES, IDEAS & VALUES). His interactions with Scrooge become increasingly sorrowful and hostile as his time on earth diminishes. Indeed, the warning he offers when he presents Want and Ignorance to the miser is laden with foreboding, condemning humanity for its bitter neglect and once again implicating Scrooge in the children's penury.

Tiny Tim Cratchit

Key quotes

'He told me, coming home, that he hoped the people saw him in the church, because he was a cripple, and it might be pleasant to them to remember upon Christmas Day, who made lame beggars walk and blind men see.' (p.80)

'God bless Us, Every One!' (p.118).

Although for many modern-day readers Tiny Tim is unbearably pious and sentimental, he appealed greatly to the Victorian reader. Tim is one of several impossibly pure children who appear in Dickens' work. His counterparts include Oliver Twist and Little Nell in *The Old Curiosity Shop*. Tim appears only briefly in the story, but he is one of several children who move Scrooge to pity and remorse, particularly in the scene following his death, where his little crutch sits by itself in the chimney corner (p.82). Tim provides an important contrast to Want and Ignorance, demonstrating that it is possible for a child to be both poor and virtuous. Importantly, this uncomplaining yet sickly boy is given the final words of the narrative, which are often identified with the story, even by those who have not read it. His primary role, though, is to personalise Scrooge's unpleasant philosophy and to make him understand that the 'surplus population' is comprised of individual human faces.

Want and Ignorance

Key quotes

'Beware them both, and all of their degree, but most of all beware this boy, for on his brow I see that written which is Doom, unless the writing be erased.' (p.94)

Like Tiny Tim, Want and Ignorance only make a brief appearance in the narrative, but they mark an important shift in its tone, as the Ghost of Christmas Past becomes sterner and more judgmental. Scrooge may be moved by the extreme pathos surrounding Tiny Tim and his brave struggle against illness, but he finds it impossible to say anything positive about these 'scowling, wolfish' figures (p.92). Want and Ignorance are not fully 'rounded' characters, in that we learn nothing about their personalities or psychology. Their role is much more overtly allegorical than that of any of the other characters and they act as an important warning, both to Scrooge and to the reader, of the race of children who will grow into hungry, resentful predators unless social reform takes place urgently. Want and Ignorance are the frighteningly ugly face of nineteenth-century poverty.

Mrs Cratchit

Key quotes

'It should be Christmas Day, I am sure … on which one drinks the health of such an odious, stingy, hard, unfeeling man as Mr. Scrooge.' (p.83)

Although a minor character, Mrs Cratchit provides a counterpoint to her husband's cheery naivety. She is a realist, who understands Scrooge for the miser he is and who clearly harbours some resentment regarding Bob's loyalty to him. Mrs Cratchit is a loving mother, who runs her household carefully; she is able to stretch the insufficient ingredients available to her in order to make a pudding that is delicious, although not really sufficient to feed a hungry family. She is strong and controlled, refusing to admit that she is crying in the vision showing her home after Tim's death, and wishing to spare Bob the sight of her 'weak eyes' for fear of upsetting him further (p.105).

The Ghost of Christmas Yet to Come

Key quotes

'Although well used to ghostly company by this time, Scrooge feared the silent shape so much that his legs trembled beneath him …' (p.95)

The silence of the final spirit is in direct contrast to the outspokenness of the Ghost of Christmas Present, suggesting that Dickens had thought carefully about the amount of social criticism that could legitimately appear in a Christmas story. It also makes the Ghost of Christmas Yet to Come the most terrifying of Scrooge's visitors. The Ghost's silence also forces Scrooge to scrutinise himself and the scenes he is observing, giving voice to his shortcomings and finally identifying himself as the figure on the bed, whose death is celebrated rather than mourned. The Ghost's dependence on a limited range of gestures (we cannot see his face, so there are no expressions for us to draw upon) makes Scrooge nervous, and as readers we share his discomfort. Instead of presenting a detailed description of his horrendous appearance, Dickens provides a blank space onto which we can project our worst nightmares.

Whereas the previous ghost's tone shifted through the visitation, beginning with jollity and ending with dire warnings, the minimalism with which Dickens depicts the Ghost of Christmas Past relieves the narrative of its didactic tone, leaving Scrooge and the reader to supply their own condemnatory words. As Scrooge becomes more vocal in his terror, so the need for the narrator to make judgmental remarks is reduced. The silences in this novella are just as important as the scenes that are filled with conversation, and the subtlety with which this spirit implicates the reader, while simultaneously evoking our sympathy for Scrooge, reveals a fascinating balance on Dickens' part between moralising and leaving readers to draw their own conclusions.

THEMES, IDEAS & VALUES

Benthamite philosophies and Malthusian economics

Although *A Christmas Carol* is primarily perceived as a ghost story, it is also a damning indictment of the inertia of the British government and public in the 1840s and their failure to respond to widespread poverty and suffering. Ebenezer Scrooge is, of course, an extreme example of the self-interest that Dickens sought to attack. The majority of readers would certainly not have identified themselves with the miserable miser. The story is, though, underpinned by a wider ideological critique through which Dickens lashes out at the greed and selfishness that he saw as one of the unfortunate characteristics of his period. In particular, he hoped to expose the self-interest underlying the government's failure to bring about widespread social reform and address the devastating effects of poverty in Britain's growing industrial cities.

Dickens uses *A Christmas Carol* to attack the Utilitarian philosophy of Jeremy Bentham (1748–1832), most notably his belief in the 'greatest happiness of the greatest number', a position that was used to justify the centralisation of Poor Relief in workhouses. Dickens, through Scrooge, also lambasts the work of Thomas Malthus (1766–1834), who argued in his *Essay on the Principle of Population* that the world could not sustain a large population and that famine and disease should be regarded as a form of natural intervention to prevent overpopulation. For Malthus, a small and affluent society was more desirable than a large population across which resources would be stretched. While in the abstract these ideas might seem logical, when applied to suffering individuals, like the Cratchit family, their underlying brutality becomes obvious. Malthus' ideas are repeated throughout the novella, first by Scrooge when he asks the portly gentleman, 'Are there no prisons?' (p.38) and suggests that the poor die to 'decrease the surplus population' (p.39). Later, the Ghost of Christmas Present repeats Scrooge's words to him, shaming him with this reminder of his lack of empathy and compassion.

Food and shopping

A Christmas Carol is brimming with descriptions of food. It is important for us to remember, as readers, that in a world where many working people suffered from malnutrition or illnesses stemming from the absence of vitamins and other dietary staples, food was a more important part of a celebration than it is today. The novella's virtuous characters are figures like Bob Cratchit and Old Fezziwig, who share food with others and enjoy it, even though it may be scarce.

Scrooge, on the other hand, does not consume food for pleasure. His dinner is 'melancholy' and eaten in a tavern, rather than prepared at home. It is striking that the narrator, who pays such close attention to what other characters are eating, does not take the time to describe Scrooge's supper, suggesting that it is as austere and unpleasant as the man engaged in eating it. Later, when he returns home, he treats his head-cold by feeding himself a saucepan of gruel, a thin porridge often served in workhouses to the poorest of the poor.

Curiously, when Scrooge tries to dismiss his initial visions of Marley's ghost, he blames his diet: 'You may be an undigested bit of beef, a blot of mustard, a crumb of cheese, a fragment of an underdone potato. There's more of gravy than of grave about you, whatever you are!' (p.45). Food for Scrooge is not so much nourishment as a cause of discomfort, and it is clear that his diet is functional rather than a source of pleasure. Indeed, when complaining to his nephew about Christmas revellers, Scrooge comments that 'every idiot who goes about with "Merry Christmas" on his lips, should be boiled with his own pudding, and buried with a stake of holly through his heart' (p.36), displaying a hostility towards his fellow men and the fare with which they celebrate the yuletide.

The other characters in the novella equate food with hospitality and companionship, and while the working poor may not have very much food, the narrator shows them making the most of it. Many of the story's depictions of food cut across class, showing that from the highest to the lowest, all are making an effort to prepare and serve the very best food they can afford:

> The brightness of the shops where holly sprigs and berries crackled in the lamp-heat of windows, made faces ruddy as they

> passed. Poulterers' and grocers' trades became a splendid joke: a
> glorious pageant, with which it was next to impossible to believe
> that such dull principles as bargain and sale had anything to do.
> The Lord Mayor, in the stronghold of the mighty Mansion House,
> gave orders to his fifty cooks and butlers to keep Christmas as a
> Lord Mayor's household should; and even the little tailor, whom
> he had fined five shillings on the previous Monday for being
> drunk and blood-thirsty in the streets, stirred up tomorrow's
> pudding in his garret, while his lean wife and the baby sallied
> out to buy the beef (pp.39–40).

In this vivid description, the narrator captures the magic of the shops, lit up for Christmas. The bright stores become an attractive spectacle for those who cannot afford their contents and, importantly, the virtuous poor whom we meet in A Christmas Carol are content to be observers of the goods that they cannot afford. While the Mayor's Christmas celebrations are lavish, there is no sense of envy on the part of the little tailor, who is happy to be stirring his pudding, in spite of his wife's ominous leanness.

Shops become an important part of the Christmas scene and those who are unable to purchase are shown with their mouths 'water[ing] gratis' as they pass by. When Scrooge and the Ghost of Christmas Past hurry to Fezziwig's warehouse, the narrator comments on the bright streets and the shops that are dressed for Christmas (p.61), while in Stave Three (pp.75–77), Dickens offers an extended description of fruit, poultry and luxury goods on display in shop windows. In this scene, the shopping is hurried, but pleasant, and the activity rapidly gives way to worship, as the people acquire their provisions and flock to Church.

These scenes, in which the poor admiringly gaze at what they cannot afford without coveting it are in direct contrast to the revolting, decayed shops Scrooge sees when he and the Ghost of Christmas Yet to Come journey to a slum area to observe the dealer in second-hand goods. Here, the shops are anything but magical; the narrator describes them as 'wretched', emphasising the enormous gap between the rich and the poor:

> Far in this den of infamous resort, there was a low-browed, beetling
> shop, below a pent-house roof, where iron, old rags, bottles,

bones, and greasy offal, were bought. Upon the floor within, were piled up heaps of rusty keys, nails, chains, hinges, files, scales, weights, and refuse iron of all kinds. Secrets that few would like to scrutinise were bred and hidden in mountains of unseemly rags, masses of corrupted fat, and sepulchres of bones (p.98).

Instead of displaying succulent meats and luscious fruit, this shop is almost decomposing, piled up as it is with used objects that are gradually breaking down. Nothing on display is tempting or desirable, and the shop represents the utter desperation that drives its clients to buy and sell its revolting contents. While this horrific emporium is a warning to Scrooge, it is also a more subtle reminder to the comfortable reader of the hellish living conditions just across the city, creating children like the predatory Want and Ignorance.

Childhood, memory and nostalgia

In recent years, critics have begun to examine the importance of memory across Dickens' writing, particularly when he depicts families and children. Michael Slater has taken this idea a step further, suggesting in his Introduction, for Dickens, Christmas and the past were inextricably bound to one another (p.xv). Certainly, memory and nostalgia are prominent concerns for Ebenezer Scrooge, who can only be reintegrated into the wider community once he has remembered his past and what it was to be a child. The centrality of memory reflects, perhaps, Dickens' own recollections of his difficult childhood, his brush with penury and his feelings of abandonment when he was sent out to the world of work as a young boy.

Rosemarie Bodenheimer has made the convincing argument that while Dickens was deeply moved by the plight of child labourers, he was also challenged by them and responded in a highly complex manner. Dickens was famous for the way in which he used his novels to raise awareness of social issues, particularly the abuse and exploitation of children. Yet Bodenheimer has pointed out that Dickens may not have fully understood his reactions to the conditions endured by young, uneducated children. Drawing on Dickens' inability to produce a factual exposé of the conditions of children employed in mines and factories that he had promised to write for the *Edinburgh Review*, Bodenheimer suggests that Dickens may have been unwittingly traumatised by the reports and illustrations emerging from the investigative commission, tasked with improving the lives of child labourers. As Bodenheimer puts it,

> The drawings of small children laboring alone in dark mines and the testimonies of uneducated young voices led on by questions from grand commissioners may have touched him painfully, perhaps in ways he did not fully understand (Bodenheimer, pp.62–3).

She goes on to argue that Dickens' reluctance to fulfil his promise was characteristic of a lifelong unwillingness to write about children who worked outside of the home. Dickens eventually justified his failure to produce the article (he later pledged that he would write a hard-hitting pamphlet, but this never appear either) by arguing that intervention in the lives of working children might lead to a reduction of family income, which could then result in starvation. Bodenheimer explicitly connects Dickens' childhood memories with his inertia on this important issue when she argues, 'His anti-protectionist stance may have served to protect his own memory against the shame of his childhood employment, by constructing the family past as a story of economic necessity' (p.63).

Malcolm Andrews has argued that Scrooge's decline begins when he loses the ability to appreciate Christmas as a child would. Part of the work performed by the ghosts, notably their return to Scrooge's childhood is, then, about helping Scrooge to recapture this more innocent, community-minded version of himself. When he awakes to find himself clutching a bedpost, rather than the bony finger of the most fearsome of the three spirits, Scrooge declares, 'I am as light as a feather, I am as happy as an angel, I am as merry as a school-boy' (p.111). This uncharacteristic expression of joy points to Scrooge's rediscovery of the meaning of Christmas as well as an ability to take himself less seriously.

The Dickensian version of Christmas involves returning to a state of childhood innocence and generosity, in which divisions between social groups can be, for a time at least, erased. Andrews has argued that both Old Fezziwig and Bob Cratchit exemplify Dickens' ideal of Christmas, even though they come from different material backgrounds:

> Fezziwig and Bob Cratchit demonstrate that, whatever one's station in life, one can assume the familial and professional responsibilities of manhood without forfeiting childlike values. Christmas, according to the tradition that Dickens inherited and revived, highlights the opportunity for a harmonious integration of these roles. It is a joyous celebration of the levelling of social and generational distinctions, and it offers adults a ritualised, licensed liberation of the spirit of childhood (Andrews, p.111).

Both Fezziwig and Bob are able to become like children for the festive season. Bob may be occupied with providing for his family and taking care of his fragile young son, Tiny Tim, yet these anxieties do not prevent him from behaving boyishly when he leaves the office or when he plays with his children. The Christmas festivities provide him with some relief from his dreary day-to-day existence and, importantly, they allow him to celebrate his faith and to give thanks for the things he values, most notably his loving and grateful dependents.

Festivity and the family

Alongside its important social and political agendas, *A Christmas Carol* is primarily a festive tale designed for holiday readers and the holiday market, with the intention of spreading good cheer. John O. Jordan has described the novella as 'something between and folktale and a modern myth' (Jordan, p.487) an evaluation that neatly encapsulates the story's enduring qualities and the place it has assumed in Christmas celebrations across the globe. In writing his obituary of Dickens, the poet Theodore Watts-Dunton famously recounted walking down Drury Lane in London in 1870 and hearing a young barrow-girl ask, 'Dickens dead? Then will Father Christmas die too?' This anecdote points to the way in which Dickens had, through a sequence of annual Christmas books, made himself synonymous with the festive season. However, it also draws attention to the cross-class appeal of Dickens' writing – there are surely not many other nineteenth-century novelists whose names would have been instantly recognisable to street vendors.

Catherine Waters has commented that 'the extent to which the shape and popularity of the Victorian Christmas might be attributed to the influence of Dickens can only be conjectured' (Waters, p.60). Tara Moore is somewhat more resolute on the question of Dickens' role and of the Victorians more generally, suggesting that while Dickens may have led the way in publishing Christmas stories and disseminating ideals of the perfect Christmas, the Victorians 'only shaped and amplified the celebration' (Moore, p.4). For the Victorians, Christmas was an important time for asserting national unity and a common humanity. According to Malcolm Andrews, the celebration of Christmas saw the temporary shedding of class distinctions, as employers and employees celebrated together, as they do at Old Fezziwig's ball. Christmas is, for Dickens, about bringing people together; thus, while Fezziwig's ball may only have cost three or four pounds, it would spread remarkable happiness. Equally, the Cratchits' pudding, although miniscule, is a source of great excitement and wonder to the children of the family, with Tiny Tim being taken off to the washhouse in order to hear it sing as it boils:

> Everybody had something to say about it, but nobody said or thought it was at all a small pudding for a large family. It would have been flat heresy to do so. Any Cratchit would have blushed to hint at such a thing (p.81).

The narrator here carefully balances the family's pleasure with the scarcity of provisions. As hardworking and proud people, the Cratchits would never complain about the smallness of their pudding, so the narrative voice emphasises the things they would never say or think, making the message all the more resonant than if one of the family had complained. It is the Cratchits' pride and naivety that make them both admirable and pitiable. Inadequate though this pudding may have been for the appetites of a growing family, it is presented as a source of delight, and the festivities are clearly one of the many ties that bind this tightly-knit group together.

Responsibility and community

When the story opens, Scrooge is presented as a man on the margins of his society. Having gradually separated himself from his nephew and his friends, he has forgotten about the ties of humanity that join people together. Dickens emphasises Scrooge's isolation by positioning him as an observer of his own life. This also allows the reader to understand the world from which he has cut himself off, without the need for excessive narratorial intervention.

As a character, Scrooge has to be reintegrated into the community, and his emotional responses to his memories and the visions aid him in this process. However, on a broader symbolic scale, Scrooge represents the many wealthy manufacturers in industrial Britain who have cut themselves off from their roots in the working classes to become fixated with profits and losses at the expense of compassion. Scrooge's rehabilitation occurs not only because he abandons his obsession with money, but also because he forms bonds with those around him, making friends and taking care of those who depend upon him: 'He became as good a friend, as good a master, and as good a man, as the good old city knew ...' (p.116). Through helping others, Scrooge is also shown to help himself and to live out a life that is considerably happier than his previously self-interested existence.

Dickens wants Scrooge's example to encourage his affluent, comfortable readers to engage with the troubles of those in their midst, to notice the unpleasantness of children like the allegorical Want and Ignorance, and to take action. Children lived and died on the streets in Dickens' London and the novelist sought to draw attention to their miserable lives. Increasingly, he refused to sentimentalise street children, presenting them in all their ghastly, predatory horror in a bid to shock readers into taking action. The most famous of Dickens' depictions is that of the ghastly crossing sweeper Jo, in *Bleak House* (1852–3), who has less education than a dog, carries diseases and repels almost all the characters because he is unwashed and smells.

One of Dickens' points in *A Christmas Carol* is that it is very easy to take care of a child like Tiny Tim, who is well-mannered, clean and compliant. The narrator may praise Scrooge for becoming a 'second father' (p.116) to the boy, but the truly important work is what Scrooge does when he approaches the Portly Gentleman and offers a substantial donation to his charity, which will hopefully reach those in direst need. The novella's Christmas tone means that the needs of children like Want and Ignorance are not fully addressed, but the fact that they are raised at all marks an important attempt by Dickens to make the reader ponder her or his own social responsibilities.

DIFFERENT INTERPRETATIONS

Different interpretations arise from different responses to a text. Over time, a text will give rise to a wide range of responses from its readers, who may come from various social or cultural groups and live in very different places and historical periods. These responses can be published in newspapers, journals and books by critics and reviewers, or they can be expressed in discussions among readers in the media, classrooms, book groups and so on. While there is no single correct reading or interpretation of a text, it is important to understand that an interpretation is more than a personal opinion – it is the justification of a point of view of the text. To present an interpretation of the text based on your point of view you must use a logical argument and support it with relevant evidence from the text.

Critical viewpoints

Early responses

The fact that *A Christmas Carol* had sold over fifteen thousand copies within the first twelve months of its publication, and attracted numerous pirated editions and adaptations shows just how popular the work was with the reading public. Dickens wrote to his American friend C.C. Felton on January 2, 1844, 'Its success is most prodigious. And by every post, all manner of strangers write all manner of letters to him [note that Dickens is here writing about himself in the third person] about their homes and hearth and how this same Carol is read aloud there, and kept on a very little shelf by itself' (*Letters*: 4, 1).

While Dickens might be considered biased in his reaction to the public response, his rival, the novelist William Makepeace Thackeray, was fulsome in his praise when he reviewed the work in February 1844. He wrote:

> It seems to me a national benefit, and to every man or woman who reads it a personal kindness … As for Tiny Tim, there is a certain passage in the book regarding that young gentleman,

> about which a man should hardly venture to speak in print or in public, any more than he would any other affections of his private heart. There is not a reader in England but that little creature will be a bond of union between the author and him, and he will say of Charles Dickens ... 'GOD BLESS HIM' (Thackeray, *Miscellanies*: 5, 214).

The reviewer in *Tait's Edinburgh Magazine* concurred with Thackeray and announced, 'Mr. Dickens has here made a decided hit' (*TEM* p.135) and in the same publication, the critic Theodore Martin (writing as 'Bon Gaultier') noted, 'It is a noble book, finely felt, and calculated to work much social good. Indeed, Dickens has produced nothing which gives me so high an idea of his powers' (*TEM* p.129).

Not everyone was swept away by the story, though. While the *Christian Remembrancer* noted in January 1844 that the novella was 'a very acceptable present at this season', its reviewer went on to register offence at the narrator's comment, 'It is good to be children sometimes, and never better than at Christmas, when its mighty founder was a child himself' (*CR* p.119). Expressing indignation, the anonymous reviewer continued:

> We do not believe that Mr. Dickens is aware of the extreme irreverence of this way of speaking; but we are mistaken if numbers of his readers will not be pained by it; and we feel bold to assure him, that his expunging, or altering, the sentence in his next edition, will give general satisfaction (CR p.119).

Other critics, including the *New Monthly Magazine* attacked the book's appearance, arguing that its expensive paper and colour plates put it beyond the reach of the very people it was attempting to help.

Two interpretations

While today we identify Scrooge as the central protagonist of *A Christmas Carol* and consider the story to be a tale focused around his haunting and subsequent redemption, the work's first readers did not experience it in this way. For many Victorians, the character at the centre of the novella was the poor, yet worthy, Bob Cratchit. Bob represented the values towards which the other characters should aspire, and he was designed to invoke sympathy and pity, as well as admiration. Set against the predatory characters who steal Scrooge's belongings and the terrifying figures of Want and Ignorance, Bob represents a hard-working sector of the poor, whom Dickens particularly admired for its patient tenacity in the face of suffering and hardship. Time has changed readerly values, however, and just as some modern readers feel impatient with Tiny Tim, so Bob's character no longer seems as prominent as it did to those responding to the book in the 1840s. While giving some thought to our own historical context and positioning, it is possible to generate two very different interpretations of Bob and Scrooge's respective roles in the novella.

Interpretation 1: Bob Cratchit is the true hero of *A Christmas Carol*

A staunch defender of Christmas who is willing to speak his mind to a frighteningly gruff employer, Bob Cratchit is central to Dickens' message about Christmas and the need to think of those less fortunate. Although not a member of Scrooge's 'surplus population' (p.39), Bob is extremely poor and it is clear from the narrator's asides during the Christmas lunch scene that he is struggling to provide for his family.

In spite of his hardship, Bob is cheery and grateful for what he has. He understands the value of human love and places it high above any worldly gain, and in this respect he embodies qualities that Victorian readers would have valued highly. Family ties were of great importance during the nineteenth century, and according to the historian G.M. Young, the family was nothing less than a 'Divine institution' (Young, p.151). Bob's great love for his family is in sharp contrast to Scrooge's bachelor status and the miser's unwillingness to engage with his one surviving relative, his nephew Fred.

Bob and Scrooge are at opposite moral poles, and Dickens clearly invites us to compare their lives, showing Bob's happy penury to be preferable to Scrooge's wealthy isolation. While Scrooge takes his meals in solitude (p.41), Bob light-heartedly flings himself down the ice slide on Cornhill 'twenty times' (p.41), before racing home to play blindman's buff with his family. While Scrooge's world is defined by work and material gain, Bob is able to balance work with play. When he leaves the office he does not carry it with him, rather he allows himself to assume childish qualities, which Dickens associates with Christmas cheer.

Bob's ability to separate his working world from his domestic life identifies him with Old Fezziwig, another character of whom the narrative voice approves. Although Fezziwig is much more successful than the clerk in material terms, they both share a love of Christmas revelry and a willingness to cast off decorum when the occasion demands it. Bob's profound goodness is evident from the fact that other 'good' characters gravitate towards him and sympathise with him. Fred, for example, hopes that his annual attempts to persuade his uncle to join him for Christmas Day might result in a small legacy for the greatly maligned clerk, while in the vision of Christmas Yet to Come, he offers Bob any assistance he can give. The Ghost of Christmas Present also obviously approves of Bob and his family, dwelling as he does on their poor feast and blessing their 'four-roomed house' (p.78).

It is, however, Bob's gentleness with his crippled son, Tiny Tim that marks him as a truly exemplary character. His love for the boy is evident in that they go everywhere together when Bob is not working, and the father carries the son on his shoulder, running all the way home from Church with him (p.79). Bob understands the wisdom of children, showing that he can learn from his son when Tim tells him that he hopes the Church-goers will see that he is a cripple (p.80).

It is, however, in his mourning that Bob is truly heroic. Child mortality was an unpleasant reality across all classes in Victorian Britain, but it had a particular impact on the poor, who suffered from malnourishment and poor living conditions. In the vision of Christmas Yet to Come, Bob shows his true strength of character through his grief-stricken acceptance of Tim's death. Although the whole family feels the loss, Bob seems to miss his constant companion more than any of the other Cratchits, breaking down and sobbing, 'My little, little child!' (p.106). In spite of his despair, Bob takes comfort in his surviving family members and once again tries to learn from Tim. Rather than giving way to a selfish, insular misery, Bob draws courage from Tim's memory and uses it to bind the family together, urging his loved ones, 'I know, my dears, that when we recollect how patient and how mild he was; although he was a little, little child; we shall not quarrel easily among ourselves, and forget poor Tiny Tim in doing it' (p.107).

In nineteenth-century terms, Bob's gentle love and his selfless grief mark him as a figure to be admired and emulated. His heroism is of a quiet, industrious kind and in identifying him with the spirit of Christmas, Dickens gently puts him forward as a character of virtue and dignity.

Interpretation 2: Scrooge, not Bob, is the novella's central protagonist

Scrooge is clearly a more significant character than his clerk, on a basic level, because the novella is structured around his experience of being haunted, and because we see so much more of him than any of the other characters. While Bob remains a static character, who does not develop or change in any way, Dickens presents Scrooge as a troubled, damaged figure who has lost his moral direction through neglect, abuse and fear.

Although there is a great deal of pathos surrounding Bob's life and his character, he is not a particularly dynamic figure and he seems to lack agency. Given his age, it is unlikely that he is indentured to Scrooge (an arrangement meaning that he would be obliged to work for him for an agreed period), yet he remains in the grasping miser's employ and there is no evidence within the text to suggest that he has ever looked for another post. To the modern reader, Bob seems to be something of a martyr, as is evidenced by Mrs Cratchit's outraged response when her husband proposes a toast to Scrooge as the 'Founder of the Feast' (p.83). The narrator never explains to us why Bob remains in his position when Scrooge is an 'odious, stingy, hard, unfeeling man', and Mrs. Cratchit demonstrates that Bob is wilfully misrepresenting Scrooge as a benefactor when she reminds her husband, 'Nobody knows it better than you do, poor fellow!' (p.83). As the provider for a large family, we would expect Bob to pursue the most lucrative employment open to him, which makes his ongoing relationship with Scrooge something of a mystery.

Bob may seem to be cheerily optimistic, but there are times when his buoyancy is unwarranted. When reporting on Tim's thoughtful response to the Church service, he declares that his son is growing 'strong and hearty' (p.80). His trembling voice shows that he clearly does not believe this statement, but wants to convince himself that it is true, suggesting that he is unable to face the reality of Tim's condition.

Scrooge, in spite of his Benthamite pronouncements in the text's opening pages, shows an adaptability which suggests that his character is more rounded than Bob's. Moved by the visions of himself as a child, and then by the difficulties of the Cratchit family, Scrooge feels empathy and sympathy for Tiny Tim. These emotions are manifested initially in his desire to know what will happen to the boy, then later when he becomes a 'second father' (p.116) to him. While Scrooge should obviously have been aware of his clerk's circumstances before this point, his desire to make amends shows a whole-hearted commitment to changing his character and to improving his previous, intolerable behaviour.

While Bob Cratchit learns from his child, Scrooge has to revisit his own childhood and learn from himself as part of his journey to understand why he has retreated from human society. The insights into Scrooge's lonely childhood days, when he was forced to spend holidays alone at school, reveal that the young Ebenezer was a sensitive, imaginative boy (p.59) with great potential. His visions of Ali Baba and Robinson Crusoe mirror Dickens' own childhood attempts to summon up memories of favourite books after they had been sold by his parents in a bid to stave off debt. This association between the young Scrooge and his creator points to a sympathy on Dickens' part and an understanding of how scarring childhood traumas can be.

In learning from the spirits and accepting their lessons, Scrooge gradually reveals that he has had heroic potential all along. His energies have been misdirected by the fear of the world identified by his fiancée, Belle (p.65), yet his willingness to adapt and change in the light of the ghostly warnings shows a strength and flexibility of character that is never developed in Bob Cratchit. Ultimately, the constraints of the novella form seem to have restricted Dickens from exploring all of his characters' inner lives. As a result, Bob inspires sympathy and pity, yet Scrooge triumphs as the story's hero.

QUESTIONS & ANSWERS

This section focuses on your own analytical writing on the text and gives you strategies for producing high quality responses in your coursework and exam essays.

Essay writing – an overview

An essay is a formal and serious piece of writing that presents your point of view on the text, usually in response to a given essay topic. Your 'point of view' in an essay is your interpretation of the meaning of the text's language, structure, characters, situations and events, supported by detailed analysis of textual evidence.

Analyse – don't summarise

In your essays it is important to avoid simply summarising what happens in a text:

- A **summary** is a description or paraphrase (retelling in different words) of the characters and events. For example: 'Macbeth has a horrifying vision of a dagger dripping with blood before he goes to murder King Duncan'.

- An **analysis** is an explanation of the real meaning or significance that lies 'beneath' the text's words (or images, in a film). For example: 'Macbeth's vision of a bloody dagger shows how deeply uneasy he is about the violent act he is contemplating – as well as his sense that supernatural forces are impelling him to act'.

A limited amount of summary is sometimes necessary to let your reader know which part of the text you wish to discuss. However, always keep this to a minimum and follow it immediately with your analysis (explanation) of what this part of the text is really telling us.

Plan your essay

Carefully plan your essay so that you have a clear idea of what you are going to say. A plan will ensure that your ideas flow logically, that your argument remains consistent and that you stay on the topic. An essay plan should be a list of **brief dot points** – no more than half a page. It includes:

- your central argument or main contention – a concise statement (usually in a single sentence) of your overall response to the topic. See 'Analysing a sample topic' for guidelines on how to formulate a main contention.

- three or four dot-points for each paragraph indicating the main idea and evidence/examples from the text. Note that in your essay you will need to *expand* on these points and *analyse* the evidence.

Structure your essay

An essay is a complete, self-contained piece of writing. It has a clear beginning (the introduction), middle (several body paragraphs) and end (the last paragraph or conclusion). It should also have a central argument that runs throughout, linking each paragraph to form a coherent whole.

See examples of introductions and conclusions in the 'Analysing a sample topic' and 'Sample answer' sections.

The introduction establishes your overall response to the topic. It includes your main contention and outlines the main evidence you will refer to in the course of the essay. Write your introduction *after* you have done a plan and *before* you write the rest of the essay.

The body paragraphs argue your case – they present evidence from the text and explain how this evidence supports your argument. Each body paragraph needs:

- a strong **topic sentence** (usually the first sentence) that states the main point being made in the paragraph

- **evidence** from the text, including some brief quotations

- **analysis** of the textual evidence explaining its significance and **explanation** of how it supports your argument

- **links back to the topic** in one or more statements, usually towards the end of the paragraph.

Connect the body paragraphs so that your discussion flows smoothly. Use some linking words and phrases like 'similarly' and 'on the other hand', but don't start every paragraph like this. Another strategy is to use a significant word from the last sentence of one paragraph in the first sentence of the next.

Use key terms from the topic – or similes for them – throughout, so the relevance of your discussion to the topic is always clear.

The conclusion ties everything together and finishes the essay. It includes strong statements that emphasise your central argument and provide a clear response to the topic.

Avoid simply restating the points made earlier in the essay – this will end on a very flat note and imply that you have run out of ideas and vocabulary. The conclusion is meant to be a logical extension of what you have written, not just a repetition or summary of it. Writing an effective conclusion can be a challenge. Try using these tips:

- Start by linking back to the final sentence of the second-last paragraph – this helps your writing to 'flow', rather than just leaping back to your main contention straight away.

- Use similes and expressions with equivalent meanings to vary your vocabulary. This allows you to reinforce your line of argument without being repetitive.

- When planning your essay, think of one or two broad statements or observations about the text's wider meaning. These should be related to the topic and your overall argument. Keep them for the conclusion, since they will give you something 'new' to say but still follow logically from your discussion. The introduction will be focused on the topic, but the conclusion can present a wider view of the text.

Essay topics

1 How does Scrooge's recollection of his childhood bring about his reform?

2 Discuss Dickens' depictions of poverty in *A Christmas Carol*.

3 Write an essay on the significance of the festive setting in *A Christmas Carol*.

4 Consider the representation of food and its absence in *A Christmas Carol*.

5   To what extent do you regard *A Christmas Carol* as a tale of redemption?

6   Write an essay on the narrative voice of *A Christmas Carol*, paying attention to how it moves between realism, terror and humour.

7   How plausible is Ebenezer Scrooge's change of character?

8   How does Dickens express the need for widespread social reform in *A Christmas Carol*?

9   Compare and contrast the three ghosts to consider which one is the most effective in bringing about Scrooge's change of heart.

10 For the novella's original readers, Bob Cratchit was regarded as the hero. Compare and contrast Bob and Scrooge to determine which character you consider to be the more successful central protagonist.

Vocabulary for writing on *A Christmas Carol*

Allegory: A meaning that is buried within a text and often not immediately obvious to the reader. Often achieved through symbolism and metaphor, the allegory requires the reader to tease out the 'hidden' meanings. Some readers regard A *Christmas Carol* as a Christian allegory of redemption, for example. Want and Ignorance are allegorical figures, rather than traditional characters, in that they are there to represent something: in this case the worst results of human negligence.

Analepsis: More commonly known as a flashback, Scrooge experiences analepsis when the Ghost of Christmas Past shows him visions of his younger self.

Benthamism: The application of the philosophies of Jeremy Bentham (1748–1832), particularly the Utilitarian belief that society should be run to secure the 'greatest happiness of the greatest number'. Those responsible for establishing the dreaded workhouses believed that by interning paupers they were adhering to Bentham's ideals.

Malthusian Economics: Thomas Malthus (1766–1834) was a notorious figure for many Victorians. Malthus argued in his *Essay on the Principle of Population* that the population would become greater than the food available and that starvation and disease were a natural check to the process.

Prolepsis: A type of foreshadowing of what will happen in the future. The scenes in which Scrooge sees people celebrating his death are potentially proleptic, although Scrooge is given the opportunity to repent and to change the course of his future.

Sabbatarianism: The belief that Sunday should be a day of absolute rest, devoted only to worship. Dickens was a staunch opponent of Sabbatarianism and attacked it in print regularly, arguing that the poor had few enough pleasures in their lives and that to insist that they could only spend their Sundays in Church was to rob them of the rest and recreation they had earned. Scrooge attacks the Sabbatarians in Stave Three of *A Christmas Carol* when he mistakenly attributes these beliefs to the Ghost of Christmas Present.

The workhouse: An institution designed to house paupers and to deter people from depending on the state for existence. Nineteenth-century workhouses were often known as 'Bastilles' after the notorious French prison, and most people went to great lengths to avoid them. When the novella begins, Scrooge is an advocate of the workhouse, suggesting to the two gentlemen collecting for charity that those without resources should be imprisoned. Workhouses were not a uniquely Victorian phenomenon, but their use became more widespread in the wake of the *Poor Law Amendment Act of 1834*.

Analysing a sample topic

To what extent do you regard *A Christmas Carol* as a tale of redemption?
Begin by thinking about what 'redemption' might mean in the context of the text. Consider the meaning of the word redemption and ask whether you see it at work within *A Christmas Carol*. Is anyone redeemed, and if so, who are they, and how and why are they redeemed? Is this just a question about 'character', or can it be extended to consider the novella's broader allegorical framework? Is the story's context important to the question of redemption? Why might Dickens urge his readers to consider the idea of being redeemed at Christmas time?

Now that you have identified the argument you will make, think about the textual evidence you will draw upon to support your ideas.

The outline below is for an essay arguing that *A Christmas Carol* is a work of redemption; the essay's main argument or contention is clearly stated in the introduction's opening sentence.

Sample introduction

In the novella *A Christmas Carol* Dickens explores the possibilities for redemption in a man who has ostracised himself from his society. While the narrative is focused on Ebenezer Scrooge's learning experiences and his reintegration into the community, his story also forms part of a broader allegory through which Dickens invites his readers to consider Christmas as a time of renewal and hope and to think about how they themselves might redeem and be redeemed. I shall therefore begin by examining the character of Scrooge and how his redemption is brought about, before widening my discussion to consider the story's broader moral focus.

Body paragraph 1

- Consider Scrooge when we first meet him, paying particular attention to his isolation, his rejection of the Christian festival of Christmas and the values that accompany it.

- Examine scenes in which Scrooge refuses to offer help to those in need, for instance his ill-treatment of his clerk (pp.40–41) and his suggestion that paupers should be imprisoned and subject to 'The Treadmill and the Poor Law' (p.38).

Body paragraph 2

- Discuss how and why Scrooge has the potential to be redeemed.

- Consider his relationship with memories and the role they play in his reform. Pay particular attention here to the visions presented by the first ghost.

- Think too about why Scrooge has become a miser. We see this through the images of his lonely school holidays (pp.56–59); his merriment at Old Fezziwig's ball (pp.62–64); and particularly his defensive comments to Belle, when she breaks off his engagement (pp.65–66).

- Discuss how Dickens' initial depiction of Scrooge as a greedy, ruthless man softens as we gain access to the miser's memories and see the forces that have shaped him.

- Think about why Dickens might want his readers to change their attitudes toward Scrooge and why he might want us to identify with aspects of the miser's behaviour.

Body paragraph 3

- Consider how Scrooge's story might reflect a broader allegorical point.

- Pay attention to the characters who are most obviously symbolic, most notably Want and Ignorance (pp.92–3) who, like Scrooge, are abused children and who, like him, will grow up to do harm unless someone intervenes.

- Think about how the Ghost of Christmas Present's language changes towards the end of the third stave.

- Pay attention to the prophetic qualities of the language and think about how the ghost's tone changes to implicate the reader, as well as Scrooge.

- Discuss the extent to which Dickens may be asking the reader to think about her or his need to be redeemed and consider the connections between engaging in social reform and achieving redemption.

Sample conclusion

A Christmas Carol closes by showing us that even the most dreadful of misers may be redeemed if they are willing to consider the needs of others above their own. By forcing Scrooge to connect with those around him, particularly those who need his aid, Dickens redeems him from the solitude that has fostered his bitterness over the years and left him without support. The Scrooge we meet at the beginning of the work is driven by fear of poverty, yet his penny-pinching ways have cut him off from all forms of community. In this respect, and through the figures of Want and Ignorance, Dickens presents a critique of the notorious *Poor Law Amendment Act of 1834*, which discouraged the idea of community aid and punished those who fell on hard times. Dickens shows that, like Scrooge, society as a whole needs to rediscover the idea of human connection and to move away from its obsession with accumulating riches. Through his simple festive allegory, Dickens draws attention to the role individuals can play in bringing about social reform and helping the poor, pointing out that in the process they may redeem both themselves and their society.

SAMPLE ANSWER

Discuss Dickens' depictions of poverty in *A Christmas Carol*.

In *A Christmas Carol* Dickens sought not only to entertain his readers, but also to alert them to the urgent need for social reform in the Britain of the 1840s. He achieves this aim by depicting a range of different types of poverty and by inviting both Scrooge and his readers to consider how these might be relieved. In this essay I shall examine Dickens' various representations of the poor and their living conditions, paying particular attention to the differences between the 'virtuous' working poor and those on the brink of starvation.

Dickens depicts different degrees of poverty in *A Christmas Carol*. In the first instance he introduces his readers to the 'acceptable' face of penury in the form of Bob Cratchit and his family. Although they occupy only four rooms and have scarcely enough food to go around, they work hard, keep themselves clean and are virtuous and decent. The narrator's pronouncement that due to Scrooge's intervention, Tiny Tim 'did NOT die' (p.116) makes clear that the young boy's ailments were a result of a poor diet and difficult living conditions. The fact that the two young Cratchits regale one another with commentary on the goose and the Christmas pudding also suggests that these children's stomachs are empty and that they daydream about things we would take for granted.

While Bob and his family are clearly very poor – we know, for instance, that Bob earns only fifteen shillings a week – they are hardworking and have no wish to be otherwise. In this respect, they are in direct contrast to the terrifying figures of Want and Ignorance, who are introduced by the Ghost of Christmas Present. Almost wild in their appearance, these two children are of a very different type from the patient and dutiful Tiny Tim, with his declaration 'God bless Us, Every One!' (p.118). Described as 'Yellow, meagre, ragged, scowling, wolfish' (p.92), Want and Ignorance are much more confronting figures than any of the Cratchit family and they represent the true dangers behind urban poverty. The narrator tells us:

> Where angels might have sat enthroned, devils lurked; and
> glared out menacing. No change, no degradation, no perversion

of humanity, in any grade, through all the mysteries of wonderful creation, has monsters half so horrible and dread (p.92).

These figures have been robbed of their childhood and through being deprived of the very basics of existence, they have been turned into vicious predators. Underlying the Ghost's description is a warning, 'Beware them both' (p.94) which seeks to shock both Scrooge and the reader into taking them and their plight seriously.

Scrooge, as we learn from his time with the first spirit, is a character who is desperately afraid of poverty. When Belle confronts him about his changed behaviour, instead of denying it he argues that he has become wiser and seeks to explain himself by saying, 'There is nothing on which [the world] is so hard as poverty; and there is nothing it professes to condemn with such severity as the pursuit of wealth!' (p.65). Here, Scrooge encapsulates his society's hypocrisy in neglecting those in need, while sneering at those who are accumulating money. This, after all, is a society in which paupers were punished through being sent to the workhouse and in which many preferred to starve rather than call upon the authorities for aid.

Scrooge may be drawn in by his observations of the Cratchits' merry feast and the many other celebrations he witnesses with the second ghost. However, it is not their world he fears, but rather that of Want and Ignorance. Scrooge's discomfort when he travels to the 'infamous resort' (p.98) of Old Joe the pawnbroker is obvious. The narrator tells us that Scrooge has never visited this part of town before, but knows its poor reputation and emphasises the fear of any respectable citizen venturing into the area by commenting that '[s]ecrets that few would like to scrutinise were bred and hidden in mountains of unseemly rags' (p.98). This scene is an important one, as it demonstrates not only the degree to which Scrooge is disliked by all who know him, but also the terrible poverty that drives people to rob the dead. The ghastly pestilence of the slums and their 'half-naked, drunken, slipshod, ugly' (p.98) inhabitants reveals a world in which nobody can be expected to prosper or live a decent life.

Dickens understood that while readers were able to identify with sentimentalised versions of poverty designed to avoid offence, the divisions within his society were simply too great. In moving from the world of the Cratchits to the vicious world of the London slums, Dickens hoped to shock those with power, like his middle-class readers, into understanding that the needs of the underclass on their doorstep had to be addressed as a priority. Continued negligence would result in the type of 'Doom' prophesied by the Ghost of Christmas Present and a probable uprising against those who ignored the poverty all around them.

REFERENCES & READING

Text

Dickens, Charles 2003, *A Christmas Carol and Other Christmas Writings*, Penguin, London.

Further Reading

Andrews, Malcolm 1994, *Dickens and the Grown-Up Child*, Macmillan, Basingstoke.

Anon, 'Notices of Books' in *The Christian Remembrancer: A Quarterly Review*, vol 7, January 1844, pp. 113–121.

Bodenheimer, Rosemarie 2007, *Knowing Dickens*, Cornell University Press, Ithaca & London.

Chesterton, G.K. 2007, *Charles Dickens*, Wordsworth Literary Lives, Wordsworth Classics, Herts.

Fielding, K.J. (ed) 1960, *The Speeches of Charles Dickens*, Clarendon Press, Oxford.

Guida, Fred 1999, *A Christmas Carol and its Adaptations*: *Dickens' Story on Screen and Television*, McFarland & Co, Jefferson, NC.

Jaffe, Audrey March 1994, 'Spectacular Sympathy: Visuality and Ideology in Dickens' *A Christmas Carol*', PMLA 109: 2, pp.254–265.

John, Juliet 2011, *Dickens and Mass Culture*, Oxford University Press, Oxford.

Jordan, John 2008, 'Postcolonial Dickens' in David Paroissien (ed), *A Companion to Charles Dickens*, Blackwell, Oxford, pp. 486–500.

Martin, Theodore, 'Bon Gaultier and His Friends' in *Tait's Edinburgh Magazine*, vol 6, December 1844, pp. 119–131.

Miller, J. Hillis Winter 1993, 'The Genres of *A Christmas Carol*' in *The Dickensian*, vol 89, pp. 193–203.

Moore, Tara 2009, *Victorian Christmas in Print*, Palgrave Macmillan, Houndsmill, Basingstoke.

Parker, David 2006, *Christmas and Charles Dickens*, AMS Press, New York.

Patten, Robert L. 1971, 'Dickens Time and Again', in *Dickens Studies Annual*, vol 2, pp. 163–196.

Schlicke, Paul (ed.) 1999, *The Oxford Reader's Companion to Charles Dickens*, Oxford University Press, Oxford.

Smith, Sheila M. 1980, *The Other Nation: the Poor in English Novels of the 1840s and 1850s*, Clarendon Press, Oxford & New York.

Slater, Michael 2009, *Charles Dickens*, Yale University Press, New Haven.

Stone, Harry 1999, '*A Christmas Carol*: Giving Nursery Tales A Higher Form' in *The Haunted Mind: The Supernatural in Victorian Literature*, Elton E. Smith and Robert Haas (eds), Scarecrow, Lanham, MD, and London, pp.11–18.

Thackeray, William Makepeace 1855–1857, *Miscellanies: Prose and Verse, Volume V,* Bradbury & Evans, London. (Reprint of review from *Fraser's Magazine*, February 1844.)

Thomas, Deborah A. 1982, *Dickens and the Short Story*, University of Pennsylvania Press, Philadelphia.

Waller, John 2005, *The Real Oliver Twist, Robert Blincoe: A Life that Illuminates an Age*, Icon Books, London.

Waters, Catherine 1997, *Dickens and the Politics of the Family*, Cambridge University Press, Cambridge.

Wilson, Edmund 1929 (repr. 1941), 'Dickens: The Two Scrooges', in *The Wound and the Bow: Seven Studies in Literature,* Riverside Press, Cambridge, MA, pp.1–104.

Young GM 2007, *Victorian England: Portrait of an Age*, Oxford University Press, Oxford.

Adaptations

There have been countless adaptations of *A Christmas Carol* on the stage, radio, television and big screen, some including the cast of *Sesame Street* and well-known Disney characters like Mickey Mouse and Donald Duck. So popular is Dickens' novella that there are also numerous annual readings in the month of December; one of the most famous is by Dickens' descendant, Gerald Charles Dickens. The story is also updated, parodied or pastiched regularly. The titles below offer a starting point for those interested in adaptations, but the list is by no means exhaustive.

Film

It's a Wonderful Life, 1946, dir. Frank Capra, Liberty Films, screenplay by Frank Capra, Frances Goodrich, Albert Hackett and Jo Swerling. Starring James Stewart, Donna Reed, Lionel Barrymore. Although based on Philip Van Doren Stern's short story, 'The Greatest Gift' (1943), many critics and viewers regard this movie as an attempt to transpose *A Christmas Carol* into a North American context. The director, Frank Capra, imports a number of Dickensian motifs into the story.

Scrooge, 1951, dir. Brian Desmond Hurst, United Artists, screenplay by Noel Langley. Starring Alistair Sim, Mervyn Johns and Hermione Baddeley. A very popular adaptation.

Scrooge, 1970, dir. Ronald Neame, Cinema Center Films, screenplay by Leslie Bricusse. Starring Albert Finney and Alec Guinness. A musical adaptation of the novel, which remarkably manages to convey some of the terror of Dickens' original writing.

Scrooged, 1988, dir. Richard Donner, Paramount Pictures, screenplay by Mitch Glazer and Michael O'Donaghue. Starring Bill Murray. An attempt to update Dickens' story, situating it within the context of 1980s corporate greed.

A Christmas Carol, 2009, dir. Robert Zemeckis, Walt Disney Pictures, screenplay by Robert Zemeckis. Starring Jim Carrey, Gary Oldman and Colin Firth. A three-dimensional, computer animated adaptation that is very faithful to Dickens' original story. The fact that this is Disney's third adaptation of the novella indicates the *Carol*'s enduring popularity.

Websites

There are many websites devoted to the work of Charles Dickens, but you should exercise caution when using them for study purposes. Try to restrict yourself to sites administered by academic organisations and libraries wherever possible.

http://dickens.ucsc.edu/

Ever-expanding resources for students and teachers working on Dickens.

http://www.victorianweb.org/authors/dickens/xmas/pva33.html

A helpful scholarly site with a discussion of the Christmas books and an extended bibliography.

http://special.lib.gla.ac.uk/exhibns/month/dec1999.html

Link to reproductions of the original colour engravings to accompany Dickens' text, with commentary from the Special Collections librarians at the University of Glasgow.

http://charlesdickenspage.com/carol-dickens_reading_text.html

A link to a copy of Dickens' script for his highly popular public readings of A Christmas Carol. This script was condensed by Dickens.

notes